WHEN THE BUCK STOPS WITH YOU

PORTFOLIO

WHEN THE BUCK STOPS WITH YOU

Harry S. Truman on Leadership

ALAN AXELROD

PORTFOLIO

PORTFOLIO
Published by the Penguin Group
Penguin Group (USA) Inc., 375 Hudson Street, New York, New York 10014, U.S.A.
Penguin Books Ltd, 80 Strand, London WC2R 0RL, England
Penguin Books Australia Ltd, 250 Camberwell Road, Camberwell,
Victoria 3124, Australia
Penguin Books Canada Ltd, 10 Alcorn Avenue, Toronto, Ontario, Canada M4V 3B2
Penguin Books India (P) Ltd, 11 Community Centre, Panchsheel Park,
New Delhi—110 017, India
Penguin Books (N.Z.) Ltd, Cnr Rosedale and Airborne Roads,
Albany, Auckland, New Zealand
Penguin Books (South Africa) (Pty) Ltd, 24 Sturdee Avenue,
Rosebank, Johannesburg 2196, South Africa

Penguin Books Ltd, Registered Offices: 80 Strand, London WC2R 0RL, England

First published in 2004 by Portfolio, a member of Penguin Group (USA) Inc.

1 3 5 7 9 10 8 6 4 2

Copyright © Alan Axelrod, 2004
All rights reserved

LIBRARY OF CONGRESS CATALOGING-IN-PUBLICATION DATA
Axelrod, Alan, 1952–
    When the buck stops with you : Harry S. Truman on leadership / Alan Axelrod.
    p. cm.
    Includes bibliographical references and index.
    ISBN 1-59184-028-7
    1. Truman, Harry S., 1884–1972—Views on leadership.   2. Political
leadership—United States—History—20th century.   3. United States—Politics
and government—1945–1953.   4. Presidents—United States—Biography.
I. Title.

E814.A93   2004
973.918'092—dc22   2003061422
[B]

This book is printed on acid-free paper.

Printed in the United States of America
Set in Adobe Garamond

For Anita and Ian

Acknowledgments

This book is built on the plainspoken eloquence of Harry S. Truman, but my presentation and interpretation of it have been sharpened and greatly improved by the diligent wit of two superb editors, Stephanie Land and Leni Grossman. The president would have been grateful. I know I am.

Contents

Introduction

DO YOUR DAMNEDEST

"Three things can ruin a man," Harry Truman once said, "power, money, and women. I never wanted power, I never had any money, and the only woman in my life is up at the house right now."

For once, the Man from Missouri wasn't being 100 percent honest. There *was* another woman in Truman's life. It was his daughter, Margaret, to whom he was devoted with a love at once intense and easygoing. He wrote her many letters over the years, including one in which he confessed, "Your dad will never be reckoned among the great." He continued:

> But you can be sure he did his level best and gave all he had to his country. There is an epitaph in Boot Hill Cemetery in Tombstone, Arizona, which reads, "Here lies Jack Williams; he done his damnedest." What more can a person do?

This is a book of lessons on leadership from Harry Truman. But Truman, a lover of sharp, straight, homely words, would have called them something else: lessons on doing your damnedest.

Such lessons are not easy to come by.

We are continually tempted to do less than our damnedest and, at virtually every turn, are told to pursue the quick and dirty, advised to "work smart, not hard," and urged to take the money and run. Plug away at a job or a career long enough, and it is easy to forget who you are and of what, at your truest best, you are capable. Each day, you may drift further and further from your damnedest or, even worse, you may never even discover just what your damnedest is.

Harry Truman sacrificed much. He dedicated himself to public service. He took on all the responsibility of office, every last bit of it, and accepted all the criticism, every bitter jab. At the same time, he turned away most of the praise and the credit, deflecting it to those who loyally reported to him. But one sacrifice he would never make: to do less than his damnedest. Give up your best self, choose not to stretch, take the fast, low road—these easy alternatives were much too hard for Truman.

The facts of Harry Truman's life, including those from childhood through his pre–White House political career, are surveyed in Chapter 1, "Missouri to the White House, the White House to Missouri," and what is most striking about them is that they are hardly striking at all. Truman was an admirable but, as he himself said, a perfectly ordinary man—who nevertheless resolved to do his damnedest.

This is not a learned political study or a meditation on the nature of power. It is a hard and practical look at the leadership moments in the life and career of Harry S. Truman through the lens of his own words and the words of those with whom he dealt directly. The purpose is to distill lessons that can be applied to any situation—especially in business—that requires making definitive decisions, making difficult choices, and mastering a legion of competing priorities.

Learning from example is an enterprise Truman himself heartily approved. "If I couldn't have been a pianist," he once remarked, "I think I would have done better as a professor of history."

My debt to history is one which cannot be calculated. . . . The leader of any country . . . must know the history of not only his own country but of all other great countries, and . . . he must make the effort to apply this knowledge to the decisions that have to be made. . . .

He said: "There is nothing new in the world except the history you do not know." And this he understood from a very early age. "While still a boy I could see that history had some extremely valuable lessons to teach."

The point is not that Harry Truman was a frustrated history teacher or a history buff, but that he was a history *user*, who searched for the practical lessons of the past, plucked them out, revolved them in his mind, and applied them to the present.

Why do this? Why look for precedent and blueprint in the past?

By "history," Truman meant no mere collection of dates and events, but the story of human decisions, the causes and effects of leadership. "Men," he said, "make history. History does not make men." To learn from history is to learn from leaders and the choices they made.

Truman believed that the lessons of history would not just help him to lead, but were essential to make him a leader. For he always said he was not a born leader, but an "ordinary man." Not that there was anything wrong with being an ordinary man. Far from it. "I am sure that right down in your heart you know that the ordinary man is the backbone of the country," he once told an audience of farmers. But like so many of his generation—a generation, FDR famously observed, to which little enough had been given, but from which much was expected—Truman was an ordinary man thrust into extraordinary circumstances.

Ultimately, it is the ordinariness of Harry Truman that makes him so effective a teacher of leadership. The problems he faced— the climax of World War II, the atomic bomb, the political and moral necessity of rebuilding Europe and Asia, the economic stresses of postwar America, the Cold War, the Korean War, the urgency of civil rights—were great and to all appearances overwhelming, while he, in contrast, was, well, ordinary. If Harry Truman could find *his* way and take the people with him, so, it would seem, can each of *us*, in whatever challenging enterprise we find ourselves.

As Truman built his leadership skills largely upon a foundation of historical example, so today's managers, supervisors, and CEOs can hone theirs on the hard surface of Truman's example. It's a pity he never distilled his experience into a manual of leadership. For what working manager has the luxury of time to dive into Truman's speeches, interviews, letters, and recollections to locate the leadership pearls?

This book does that job and more, presenting Truman's key observations on the style, tactics, and strategy of leadership. Each observation is examined and discussed in its historical context and distilled into a practical, immediately usable lesson. Here is the best of Harry Truman, intended to bring out the best in us.

The text is divided into a dozen chapters. The first presents a brief biography, and the next ten approach the model of Truman's leadership thematically, with lessons on

- Defining and attaining worthwhile goals
- "Riding the tiger"—enduring, surviving, and mastering your job
- Penetrating pretense (i.e., cutting through the crap)
- Leading by example
- Giving hell—and taking it in return
- Creating consensus and common cause
- Making decisions
- Finding the facts—then using them effectively
- Creating ethical leadership
- Managing time

The last chapter, "Reckoning," presents Truman's own summary of what it takes to be a leader. A concluding Appendix offers "A Truman Timeline" and is followed by recommendations for further reading.

Read right, the life of Harry Truman is nothing less than a handbook of accountability. Truman kept on his desk the most famous motto any modern leader has ever adopted: THE BUCK STOPS HERE. And so this book is about becoming and being a buck stopper, achieving accountability, accepting accountability, and using it creatively: making it your motto, too, by learning how to do your damnedest every time.

WHEN THE BUCK
STOPS WITH YOU

CHAPTER 1

MISSOURI TO THE WHITE HOUSE, THE WHITE HOUSE TO MISSOURI

At 7:09 in the evening of April 12, 1945, two hours and twenty-four minutes after Franklin Delano Roosevelt succumbed to a cerebral hemorrhage while sitting for a portrait at the "Little White House" in Warm Springs, Georgia, his vice president stood in the Cabinet Room of the White House in Washington, right hand raised, left hand on the cover of the only Bible that could be found quickly, a Gideon belonging to Howell Crim, head usher of the White House. Chief Justice Harlan Stone began the oath of office, "I, Harry Shipp Truman," to which the vice president responded, "I Harry S. Truman. . . ."

Sixty-one years earlier, on May 8, 1884, in a tiny bedroom off the parlor of their home in the market hamlet of Lamar, Missouri, a boy was born to John Anderson Truman and Martha Ellen Young. It would be a month before Dr. W. L. Griffin, the physician who delivered the boy, registered the birth with the county clerk. Even then, he had no name to supply, because the parents were still debating the baby's middle name. It had certainly been decided that he would be called Harry, after his Uncle Harrison, but should his middle name honor John's father, Anderson Shipp Truman, or Martha's, Solomon Young? Ultimately, the parents compromised on the initial S, which honored both grandfathers, and that initial is quite possibly the only thing about Harry S. Truman that even approaches the level of mystery.* In all other respects, from beginning to end, his life was what he wanted it to be: an open book, clearly, simply, and honestly written.

---

*Some sticklers for grammar and logic insist the S be used without punctuation because it stands for nothing other than itself. Truman, however, habitually used the period in his signature, and so I will use it here.

Harry's father was a mule trader and farmer, and when the mule business became sluggish, he moved the family from Lamar to a farm near Harrisonville in 1885 and then to another farm, near Grandview, in 1887. Nearsighted—he would get his first pair of glasses at age nine—and slight of build, Harry Truman was not cut out to be a farmer, so it was just as well that the family, which now included another boy, John Vivian Truman (always called Vivian), moved to Independence in 1890. It was there that a sister, Mary Jane, was born, and it was there that most of Harry's schooling took place.

He was, in fact, a rather bookish child. Unable to see well without his glasses, he always wore them; very much aware that they were expensive, he was fearful of breaking them in rough play. "To tell the truth," the painfully truthful Truman confessed in later life, "I was kind of a sissy." His brother's assessment was far kinder. True, Harry was not a scrapper, but, Vivian insisted, he commanded a "lot of respect" from the other boys, who actually admired the store of knowledge he amassed about such exciting subjects as former Missourians Jesse James and the Dalton gang.

Harry most enjoyed reading and playing the piano, in that order, and, as he grew into adolescence, he thought about a career as a historian or a pianist. However, John Truman was never sufficiently successful as a farmer or a businessman to finance a college education or advanced musical training for Harry, who, after graduating from high school in 1901, briefly attended business college and worked for two weeks in the mail room of the *Kansas City Star*. Next, he became a timekeeper for a Santa Fe Railroad construction project and, in 1903, found work as a bank clerk and then as a bank bookkeeper in Kansas City. Even in this prosaic employment, he did his very best—his "damnedest"—and received high praise from his supervisors. Doubtless he would have risen in the bank, but, in 1905, he was summoned to the family's new farm at Blue Ridge, near Grandview. Its 600 acres were too much for John Truman and Vivian to handle on their own, and so, like it or not, Harry Truman finally became a farmer. And when his father died in 1914, that vocational destiny seemed sealed as the farm fell to him.

There is not the slightest indication that the more or less enforced return to the farm created any resentment in Harry Truman. Indeed, running a farm gave him the air of sufficient substance to justify, in his own mind, courting Elizabeth—Bess—Wallace in earnest. That courtship began about 1911, but Harry had been sweet on Bess ever since he had first met her in 1890 at the Sunday school of Independence's First Presbyterian Church. Still, it would be November 1913 before the couple became engaged, secretly. By the beginning of 1917, they were about ready to get married at last, but in April the United States entered World War I, and Truman, who did not want to risk making a widow of Bess, postponed the marriage. At thirty-three, he was beyond draft age, and no one expected him to serve, but, bad eyesight and all, he saw his duty, volunteered, and was sent to France in 1918 as the captain of a field artillery unit that engaged in hot and hazardous action at Saint–Mihiel and the Meuse–Argonne.

Truman never acquired a taste for military life, but, as the officer in charge of a company of men, he did learn what it meant to be a leader, and he found he had an aptitude for leadership as well as an affinity for the responsibility it brought. Nevertheless, when he was mustered out and returned to Missouri in 1919, it was not a leadership position he sought. After marrying Bess Wallace, he opened a haberdashery on Kansas City's 12th Street in partnership with an army buddy, Eddie Jacobson. To a newly married man, it seemed the financially responsible thing to do, and, at first, he and Jacobson did quite well.

Very likely, Harry Truman would have spent his life as a Kansas City businessman had the shop not foundered in the postwar recession of the early 1920s. Out of business, deeply in debt, newly married, and now without a clear direction in life,

Truman accepted a friend's introduction to Thomas J. "Boss" Pendergast, Democratic nabob of the Kansas City political machine. No one got very far in Missouri politics without a nod and a boost from Pendergast and his minions, whose machine was at once an economic boon to Kansas City and a municipal source of national disgrace—for it was during the Pendergast years that the town earned its reputation for officially sanctioned vice and racketeering.

Backed by Pendergast, Truman won election as county judge in 1922, lost a reelection bid in 1924, but was elected presiding judge of the county court in 1926. Despite its title, this office was not judicial, but administrative. Truman functioned as county commissioner, effectively chief executive of Jackson County, Missouri. Astounding to all involved, this latest Pendergast protégé, during two four-year terms, built a reputation for scrupulous honesty, selfless public stewardship, and skillful, no-nonsense management that was instantly and impartially responsive to the needs of the people. Under Judge Truman, Jackson County got modern and efficient highways and badly needed public buildings, all contracted for and constructed without the favoritism and corruption customary in Pendergast's Missouri.

Truman was well aware of T. J. Pendergast's reputation, and he was even more aware that most of the bad things said about "TJP" were amply merited; however, throughout his long political career, Truman never repudiated or even criticized his first mentor, and he pointed out that Pendergast never interfered with him or compelled him to do anything to compromise his own integrity. Nevertheless, as it became clear to Boss Pendergast that Harry Truman was hardly a team player, the odds of the machine's backing him for further and higher political office became increasingly remote. Because two terms marked the traditional limit for a presiding county judge, it seemed to Truman, in 1934, that his political career had reached its end. He accurately predicted that Pendergast would tap others to run in the Democratic primary for a seat in the U.S. Senate, but what he had not counted on was that no one else wanted the job. After several turndowns from others, Pendergast finally turned to Truman.

If Truman felt the slightest resentment at having been far from Pendergast's first choice, he showed none of it in his vigorous campaign. He won the Democratic primary, which, in the "Solid South" Missouri of those days, was tantamount to winning the election. It is true that when he entered the Senate in 1935 he did so under the cloud of Pendergast corruption, but his open-handed, plainspoken friendliness, frank integrity, and commitment to his office quickly won respect, trust, and, not least of all, affection from colleagues and public alike. While he compiled a modest but efficient record of achievement during his first Senate term, it was during his second term that he entered the national spotlight by creating and chairing a committee charged with uncovering waste and fraud in the U.S. military and its suppliers.

Prodded by its chairman, the Truman Committee, as it was informally and universally called, was ruthless in holding military officers, civil administrators, and—especially—defense contractors to the highest standards of efficiency, performance, and value for money. Yet Truman was far less interested in punishing poor performers or even outright frauds than in motivating them to deliver what they were supposed to and what they had promised. To that end, the Truman Committee made it a practice to issue draft reports of its findings to the corporations, unions, and government agencies under investigation, thereby inviting voluntary correction of abuses before prosecution was commenced.

Almost always, this proved abundantly persuasive. In one famous instance, on the eve of World War II, Truman challenged aviation manufacturer Glenn Martin to redesign the B-26 bomber after it had gone into production with wings that were simply too short to achieve adequate performance. Worse, the design flaw posed a safety hazard that had already sent several airmen to their deaths. In testimony before the committee, Martin told Truman that the design was already on the boards and in production, so that it was too late to make changes. Truman responded with typical directness that "if the lives of American boys depended upon the planes that were produced for the United States Army Air Force the committee would see to it that no defective ships were purchased." This elicited a single sentence in reply from Martin: "Well, if that's the way you feel about it, we'll change it."

Truman's Senate record made him an attractive candidate for FDR's running mate in his fourth-term campaign of 1944. Truman, however, loved the Senate and had no burning desire to become the nation's vice president. He staunchly resisted the nomination until Roosevelt, desperately seeking an alternative to the current vice president, Henry A. Wallace (perceived as too left wing), and to Office of War Mobilization head James F. Byrnes (too ambitious), angrily insisted. Over the phone, FDR gave Democratic Party worker Robert Hannegan a message for Truman: "You tell the senator that if he wants to break up the Democratic Party in the middle of the war, that's his responsibility." As the *bang* of a slammed receiver echoed in Hannegan's ear, he relayed the message to Truman verbatim and, as some recalled, the senator uttered only two monosyllables in response: "Oh, shit!" Truman himself remembered a different reply: "Well, if that's the situation, I'll have to say yes."

During the eighty-two days of his service in the Roosevelt administration, Truman met with FDR only twice. The president never formally briefed his vice president, let alone counseled, groomed, or in any way prepared him. Of the existence of the atomic bomb project, for instance, Truman was told absolutely nothing.

And so, on April 12, 1945, Truman's elevation to the presidency came under the worst possible circumstances: under cover of the ignorance in which FDR had kept him and upon the sudden death of a larger-than-life four-term chief executive, the man who had led the nation through the Depression and through the darkest, hardest days of World War II, a leader who came as close to being worshiped by his people as any American president ever has. At Roosevelt's death, victory had been all but completely won in Europe, but the Pacific war raged on. The Missourian found himself thrust among top generals and allied leaders who included the monumental Winston Churchill and the enigmatic Joseph Stalin.

To say that Truman "rose to the occasion" is a pallid understatement. Following a great leader in a time of unparalleled danger, the new president became a great leader in his own right. The decisions he had to make were momentous, world changing, world building, and, potentially, world destroying. Often, his decisions were unpopular. The press—the "sabotage press," Truman sometimes called it—which was overwhelmingly Republican in orientation throughout most of the country, continually sniped at him, one journalist famously quipping, "To err is Truman."

Truman didn't let it matter. He led the nation and made some of the most difficult and important decisions any president has ever made. The first and most famous, of course, was the decision to use the newly developed atomic bomb against Japan, but as consequential as that decision was, Truman later claimed that many others were far harder. Several times in the months and years following the war, he had to go against his own intensely prolabor sympathies to bring the full force of the government to bear in averting or ending coal, rail, and steel strikes that threatened to cripple the nation. In 1948, he had to overcome his own family's Confederate political roots and a white Southerner's heritage of racism to propose and implement the first significant civil rights measures since Reconstruction. That same year, he acted contrary to a number of advisers, including the Cabinet member he most admired, George C. Marshall, in making the United States the first nation to grant official recognition to the new state of Israel. Truman had to lay out a course for the "containment" of expanding Soviet and Chinese Communist aggression—and he had to do so without triggering a cataclysmic third world war. This included ordering the Berlin Airlift of 1948–1949, by which the first major "battle" of the Cold War was won, and conducting a heartbreaking and frustrating "police action" in Korea, resisting the Communist invasion of the democratic south without allowing the conflict to engulf the world.

From the generation that had come of age under Franklin Roosevelt, much had been required indeed. Yet that generation made its sacrifices in light of a vividly clear and ever-present knowledge of the evils it fought. The next generation, under Truman, was faced with a world in some ways even more terrifying, yet fraught with evils far more obscure and ambiguous, the confronting of which required an effort made all the more exhausting precisely because it had, in so many ways, to be continually and carefully restrained. Truman understood that he led a great and victorious nation on the threshold of perhaps even greater achievement. Yet he also understood that he was the first world leader who possessed the power to destroy civilization itself.

Truman was president for all but the first eighty-two days of the fourth term to which Roosevelt had been elected. His chances of getting elected in his own right were reckoned vanishingly slim by just about everyone in 1948 except Truman himself. Feeling that the Republican-dominated press would never give him a fair shake, Truman decided to carry his case directly to the people, and he embarked on a series of cross-country whistle-stop campaign tours of unprecedented duration and extent, traveling 31,700 miles in six weeks and giving 356 speeches. While the pollsters continued to discount the chances of a Truman victory, and some oddsmakers put his chances at 30 to 1, Truman knew he had connected with the people and was supremely confident. In the end, he prevailed over the favored candidate, New York governor Thomas E. Dewey, 303 electoral votes to 189, having polled 24,105,812 popular votes to Dewey's 21,970,065.

The next four years were dominated by the Cold War, the Korean War, and an anticommunist hysteria at home that threatened the continued existence of democracy itself. Truman remained steadfast at the helm, and although supporters pleaded with him to run for a second term "in his own right" (a run to which he was entitled, since the Twenty-second Amendment, ratified in 1951 and barring presidents from serving more than two terms, did not apply to the sitting president), Truman declined. While he did not approve of a constitutionally mandated two-term limit, he nevertheless believed that, except in circumstances of extreme emergency, such as those FDR had faced, a president should voluntarily restrict himself to two terms. Any more than that risked dictatorship. His precedent for this self-imposed limit was no less than George Washington and the noble Roman to whom Washington was often compared, Cincinnatus. Washington's popularity was such that he could have been president for life, but after two terms he chose to retire, a private citizen, to his beloved Mount Vernon, much as Cincinnatus had retired to his farm, relinquishing absolute rule over Rome in 458 B.C. after he had completed the job of rescuing his country from the rebellious Aequi.

In July 1945, Harry Truman enjoyed a public approval rating of 87 percent. When he left office in January 1953, his approval rating stood at a meager 31 percent. If this bothered him, he never let on. Polls to the contrary, he knew that he had "done his damnedest," and he devoted the first several years of his retirement to writing two volumes of memoirs and then to feeding his always voracious appetite for the printed word, devouring volumes of history and biography, taking time out for brisk strolls along the streets of his beloved hometown of Independence, Missouri, and maintaining an active interest in the Democratic Party and the conduct of American policy.

With each year that has passed since the end of the Truman presidency, the wisdom and rightness of most of his decisions have become increasingly apparent. Before he died, the day after Christmas 1972, Truman even had the satisfaction of seeing his critical star securely on the rise. Today, despite detractors on the far right and far left, many regard him as among the great presidents of the twentieth century and the greatest of the postwar chief executives. In the long retrospect that is history, his appeal as a leader has become irresistible.

CHAPTER 2

ESTABLISH THE OBJECTIVE

LESSON 1
DEFINITION OF A LEADER

"While still a boy I could see that history had some extremely valuable lessons to teach. I learned from it that a leader is a man who has the ability to get other people to do what they don't want to do, and like it."

—*Memoirs, Volume One: Year of Decisions*

From childhood, Truman was an avid reader of history and biography. As a boy, he formulated a simple description of a leader, which his experience as an adult only confirmed.

LESSON 2

DRAW A LINE

"I would not stand for that."

—Memoirs, Volume One: Year of Decisions

Harry Truman was a solidly prolabor politician, and as demonstrated by his veto of the 1947 Taft-Hartley Act on the grounds that it was antilabor, he was a prolabor president. However, in May 1945, when John L. Lewis, fiery leader of the United Mine Workers of America, called a coal strike, Truman drew the line. "I would not stand for that. A coal strike would seriously cripple the war effort, and we could not permit it." Lewis defied all efforts at mediation, miners at more than 300 anthracite mines struck, and Truman issued an executive order that seized the mines, putting them temporarily under government control. "The same people continued to do the work but they were now working for the government."

The seizure of the mines was hardly popular with Truman's labor constituents, and it went against the president's own grain as well: "I have never believed that the government should operate private business, but it must have the means to suppress open defiance such as John L. Lewis's."

A leader is always confronted by competing priorities and sometimes even has to face extremely hard and costly choices. The guiding principle, even in the most difficult situations, must be an unwavering focus on the overriding objectives of the organization. Truman's decision was both hard *and* simple: Nothing could be allowed to jeopardize the war effort, which, although about to end in Europe (Germany surrendered on May 8, 1945), had now to focus on Japan, an even more tenacious enemy.

When the time comes to draw a line and stand firm, be certain the ground beneath your feet is solid. Take your stand on the bedrock objectives of the organization and make those objectives the basis of your most difficult choices.

LESSON 3
PROVIDE PURPOSE

"It is our responsibility—ours, the living—to see to it that this victory shall be a monument worthy of the dead who died to win it."

—Broadcast speech following the surrender of Japan, ending World War II, September 1, 1945

"We think of those whom death in this war has hurt, taking from them husbands, sons, brothers and sisters whom they loved," Truman observed in his radio address. "No victory can bring back the faces they longed to see."

It is an important leadership function to represent and express the collective values and sentiment of the organization, but it is even more important to apply these in guidance toward key objectives. Thus Truman continued: "Only the knowledge that the victory, which these sacrifices made possible, will be wisely used can give them any comfort. It is our responsibility—ours, the living—to see to it that this victory shall be a monument worthy of the dead who died to win it." And with these words, the president laid the foundation for support of a just peace, which included the great experiment known as the United Nations and which would not repeat the terrible errors of the punitive peace that had followed World War I.

Don't just define and organize action, lead always in a way that focuses action on appropriate goals. Ensure that the group understands and feels the full, larger significance of what it has done, what it is doing, and what it has yet to do.

LESSON 4
ACQUIRE THE LEADERSHIP REFLEX

". . . the taxpayers' house at 16th & Pennsylvania Ave. . . ."

—Diary entry, September 20, 1945

Truman faithfully kept a diary during his White House years, and reading it, filled as it is with unadorned colloquial speech, makes it clear that he intended the diary not for posterity, but as a record for his own use and review. In it, therefore, he could—and did—say whatever he wanted. That is why his reference to the White House as "the taxpayers' house at 16th & Pennsylvania Ave." is so telling. This was not a clever sound bite for the benefit of the public. It was a note to himself and expressed precisely how he thought of the White House: not as *his* residence, let alone *his* palace, but as a home belonging to the people, and not just their property in spirit, but in fact.

This casual note was a spontaneous expression, the product not of careful rehearsal but of Truman's leadership reflex, a reflex that reminds a leader, twenty-four hours of every day, that he is the servant of the people he leads. His very "house" is merely rented from them. In leaders as effective as Harry Truman, such service, the objective of leadership, becomes second nature, evident in even the most offhand remark.

LESSON 5
LEARN FROM HISTORY,
DON'T BE TRAPPED BY IT

"I am not one to believe in the value of hindsight."

—*Memoirs, Volume Two: Years of Trial and Hope*

In 1946, President Truman sent George C. Marshall to China in the hope of helping the various factions contending for power there to reach a consensus that would unify the country under a noncommunist government. "There is no question that Marshall's mission failed to yield the results he and I had hoped for," Truman later wrote. However: "I am not one to believe in the value of hindsight. Whether or not I was right in sending General Marshall to China does not depend on what some think they know today. It depends only on what we were able to know in 1945. At that time the belief was general that the various elements in China could be persuaded to unify the country."

Truman studied history earnestly and voraciously, but he always did so with the intention of evaluating the present or preparing for the future. He never looked back on the past with the fond and foolish hope of somehow undoing it.

Study the past, but don't brood over it. Learn from your mistakes and those of others, but understand and accept that nothing done now will undo past mistakes.

The ability to let go of the past, without turning your back on its useful lessons, is a skill acquired through a combination of will and practice. It is a skill necessary to sustained and effective leadership.

LESSON 6
CHECK YOUR EGO AT THE DOOR

"We're going to call it the Marshall Plan."

—To presidential aide Clark Clifford, early in 1948

As Margaret Truman relates in her biography, *Harry S. Truman,* the president responded brusquely to his aide's suggestion that the extraordinary and unprecedented package of financial assistance to spur European recovery after World War II be called the Truman Plan.

"Are you crazy?" the president replied. "If we sent it up to that Republican Congress with my name on it, they'd tear it apart. We're going to call it the Marshall Plan."

Not only was Truman eager to give credit for the program to its principal architect and advocate, Secretary of State George C. Marshall, whom the president respectfully called "the great one," but also Truman understood that attaching his own name to it would poison the well, prompting a knee-jerk rejection by an adversarial Congress.

It is natural for the leader of an enterprise to take credit for major initiatives, and often such credit is justified. But it is far more important to keep your sights fixed on the true objective—*selling* the program or initiative—and if this means forgoing credit for an idea, swallow hard and do just that. Never let ego get between the organization and its objectives.

LESSON 7
THE OBJECTIVE IS THE THING

"The objective is the thing, not personal aggrandizement."

—Diary entry, May 6, 1948

"I think I've been right in the approach to all questions 90% of the time since I took over," Truman noted candidly in his diary on May 6, 1948. "I was handicapped by lack of knowledge of both foreign and domestic affairs—due principally to Mr. Roosevelt's inability to pass on responsibility. He was always careful to see that no credit went to anyone else for accomplishment. . . . The objective and its accomplishment is my philosophy, and I am willing and want to pass the credit around. The objective is the thing, not personal aggrandizement. . . ."

How many leaders can truly accept this proposition? It's not easy. Much as he admired FDR, deeming him one of the few great presidents, Truman noted at the conclusion of this diary entry that "all Roosevelts want the personal aggrandizement." And this was also the case ("Too bad," Truman noted) with two other leaders the president otherwise admired: "[Secretary of State Jimmy] Byrnes and [financier and perennial presidential adviser Bernard] Baruch also have that complex."

Truman set the bar high, the only proper place for it. The most effective leaders continually shift the spotlight from themselves and shine it instead on the objectives of the enterprise. This requires a combination of maturity, selflessness, and supreme self-confidence. The point is not that grabbing glory is unseemly, but that it misdirects the energy of the organization and misspends its collective resources.

LESSON 8
LEAD BY VALUE, NOT PRICE

"Seventeen billion dollars sounded like a huge sum, and of course it was. But compared to the financial cost alone of World War II, it seemed small."

—Memoirs, Volume Two: Years of Trial and Hope

Decisions about the allocation of money and other scant resources should be driven not by price, but by value. Price is a number with little meaning, whereas value is a ratio of cost to benefit and, therefore, holds a great deal of useful information—the kind of information that validly guides a decision.

To implement the Marshall Plan, President Truman asked Congress to appropriate $17 billion to aid in the postwar relief of Europe. In 1948 dollars, this was a huge sum, yet it was intended to purchase great value: the humanitarian relief of Europe and a peaceful means of countering and containing the postwar expansion of communism. Truman knew well that the Allies had won World War I only to lose the peace with a punitive treaty that left much of Europe economically devastated. The result was a war even more terrible than the first, a war that cost far more than $17 billion. As Truman saw it, the only alternative to winning the peace following the *second* world war was a *third* world war. This understanding revealed the price of the Marshall Plan as a great value—indeed, a bargain.

LESSON 9
KNOW WHAT YOU KNOW

"Some voices were raised in America calling for a break with the Russians. These people did not understand that our choice was only between negotiations and war. There was no third way."

—*Memoirs, Volume Two: Years of Trial and Hope*

To any of the generations that lived through any part of the five-decade Cold War between the United States and the Communist bloc, the conflict was characterized more by the continual threat of violence than by actual violence. The war may have been cold, but it was hardly silent. In place of the shooting there was talking, endless rounds of accusations and counteraccusations punctuated by typically fruitless negotiations. National frustration understandably ran high. Diplomacy seemed to be getting nowhere.

That, as Truman observed, was precisely the point. The West and the Soviets were ideologically irreconcilable. Neither side was prepared to compromise its philosophy and its conduct of government. This being the case, there really was no point to negotiation—except as an alternative to the absence of negotiation, which would be World War III. What Truman understood was that diplomacy did not have to reach a productive conclusion to succeed. The mere fact of ongoing discussion ensured the absence of war. As long as the USA and the USSR were talking, they weren't shooting.

Fully appreciating the function of diplomacy in the Cold

War, Truman was willing to keep the dialogue going, absurd, exhausting, and frustrating as it might be. This willingness required a resolve born of knowing what others did not know: that options were starkly limited to talk or to war. His resolve enabled Truman to resist the frustrated clamor for some other drastic action.

Ideally, the best course is to proceed from point A to point B, with point B representing some obviously productive outcome. In the real world, such a direct route is not always available, and sometimes you must navigate as best you can and to the best purposes you can define. This "best" may not satisfy everyone, and so leadership becomes, in part, successfully resisting a popular insistence on taking some deceptively appealing action. Maintain this resistance by always knowing what you know—and simultaneously knowing that others do *not* know what you know.

LESSON 10
KNOW WHAT TO DO WHEN
NOTHING CAN BE DONE

"I ordered no report—and there wasn't any."

> —Letter to his cousins Nellie and Ethel Noland,
> September 8, 1949

"I'll tell you a secret which you must not under any circumstances repeat," Truman wrote in a letter to his cousins. "Coming from Des Moines Tuesday, No. 4 engine on my fine plane conked out! You should have seen the scurrying and running to & fro. I sat still and watched 'em. Then we straightened out and came in on 3 engines. We were only up 6000 feet so there was no jump out and anyway I wouldn't jump until everybody else had—and it couldn't have been done at 6000. What a headline that would have made! I ordered no report—and there wasn't any."

Leadership requires identifying, defining, and prioritizing objectives, then determining the best means of achieving them, doing whatever is necessary to put those means into operation, and managing the operation until the objectives have been attained.

But sometimes it is impossible to identify any useful objective. A leader naturally wants to do *something*, whatever the situation. Sometimes, however, there is nothing useful to be done, and an effective leader must be capable of recognizing and accepting such situations without responding inappropriately or destructively—and without relinquishing leadership.

So when Harry Truman found himself aloft one day in the

Independence, the four-engine, propeller-driven DC-6 airliner that served as the presidential aircraft, and was aware an engine had failed, the best leadership course was to let the crew members take control.

But then, after the plane landed safely, an objective did emerge. To make a report of the incident, a report that would inevitably find its way into headlines, would serve no good purpose. It would, in fact, only emphasize the vulnerability of the president, something the nation did not need to be reminded of. After all, just four years earlier, the people had lost their beloved and seemingly invincible leader when FDR succumbed to a cerebral hemorrhage. It was not, therefore, personal modesty or a love of secrecy that led Truman to make the decision to order no report, but a wish to achieve the objective of protecting the presidency and avoiding any cause for public alarm.

When an engine of the *Independence* failed, there was almost nothing the president could do, but he did what he could—and absolutely no more.

LESSON 11
PUT FIRST THINGS FIRST

"It makes not much difference what sort of a building you're in when you are after knowledge, but it does count entirely on who teaches you."

—Letter to his cousin Nellie Noland, October 29, 1949

Most planners and managers are chronic sufferers of a disorder we might call the "edifice complex." They like to buy equipment and, even more, they have a passion for erecting buildings. Truman recognized this when he wrote to his Cousin Nellie about funding for education:

> My first, second and fourth grade teachers made more impression on me than all the rest put together. I skipped the third grade. They were good women who taught moral integrity as well as a.b.c.'s and readin', writin', & 'rithmetic. It makes not much difference what sort of a building you're in when you are after knowledge, but it does count entirely on who teaches you. Of course I believe in an adequate plant [school-house] too. But we've been thinking too much about the plant and not enough about what the plant is for.

In planning, begin with the objective rather than whatever shell—the physical "plant"—and appurtenances surround it. Lead toward the objective, not its empty husk.

29

LESSON 12
PLAN BIG

"Make no little plans. Make the biggest one you can think of, and spend the rest of your life carrying it out."

—*The Autobiography of Harry S. Truman*
(Robert H. Ferrell, ed.)

Too many would-be leaders confuse ambition with self-aggrandizement or just plain selfishness. Genuine ambition is too big to serve only the self. Plans that relate exclusively to oneself are not ambitious, but selfish and small, no matter how grandiose. The truly ambitious make big plans that encompass entire organizations, corporations, even nations. Large in scope, a plan should be open-ended in time, allowing for future needs and opportunities by anticipating the unanticipated. Always think beyond yourself, and that begins with the plans you make.

"You can always amend a big plan," Truman remarked in 1949, "but you can never expand a little one." A plan should be a seed, enabling growth, not a container, limiting development. "I don't believe in little plans. I believe in plans big enough to meet a situation which we can't possibly foresee now."*

*Quoted in Ralph Keyes, *The Wit and Wisdom of Harry Truman.*

LESSON 13
ECONOMIZE THE MESSAGE

"Cut your speech to twenty-five minutes, shake hands with as many people as you can for a little while. Afterward, even if you have time left, leave. If you have no place to go, you can always pull off the road and take a nap."

—Quoted in Jonathan Daniels, *The Man of Independence*

Harry Truman was known as a direct, incisive speaker, but he did not have a particular reputation for being a man of few words. He was, for example, nothing like the thirtieth president, Calvin Coolidge, whose taciturnity was sufficiently legendary to merit the nickname "Silent Cal." Of him, the humorist Will Rogers quipped, "He don't say much. But when he says something, he don't say much." Had he lived in the Truman era, Rogers could not have said this about Truman. Neither notably taciturn nor especially voluble, Truman used language with blunt economy, saying exactly what he felt had to be said and doing so with neither more nor fewer words than necessary. This tactic had a simple purpose: to communicate.

The objective of a political campaign—or any campaign of persuasion—is to sell yourself and your program. With this objective in mind, Truman determined that a speech lasting just under half an hour would provide plenty of time to get his message across without severely abridging it, on the one hand, or lulling his audience into bored inattention on the other. Moreover, the twenty-five-minute speech consumed enough time to present himself to the people while leaving sufficient time to be interactive: to wade into the crowd and shake some hands. Beyond this, Truman saw a danger of wearing out his welcome by demanding too much of a commodity as valuable to his audience as to himself: time.

Observe a strict economy in delivering your message. Make a good bargain with your audience: *Give* enough time to say what you need to say without *taking* too much time to do so.

LESSON 14
DON'T CREATE PANIC

"Of course I did not want to announce that an emergency was at hand without suggesting what we ought to do about it."

—Memoirs, Volume Two: Years of Trial and Hope

As the Korean War intensified, President Truman decided to proclaim a national emergency. This important step would allow the executive branch to marshal forces and resources on a large scale and a fast track and, if necessary, to introduce controls on prices and production. As important as proclaiming an emergency was, Truman did not want the action to trigger a panic, and the way he decided to avoid panic was to delay the proclamation until he had at the ready a set of positive measures to take in conjunction with it.

In an extreme or urgent situation, it is foolhardy to act as if nothing out of the ordinary is happening. In such a case, it is the leader's task to put the organization on alert so that it can focus its resources most effectively. But, by itself, such a call of alarm may serve only to squander energy in panic rather than concentrate it for necessary effort. If you raise the level of the group's energy, you must simultaneously identify the appropriate route for that energy to take. It is a serious mistake to call people to action without defining an action to perform. What makes the leader's task particularly difficult is that leaders are expected not only to raise the right questions, but also to reassure their organization that—at the very least—they know where to seek the answers.

Resist the temptation to rush a general announcement of crisis or bad news. First, review your options, then seek help and counsel from an inner circle of trusted advisers. Only after these two steps have suggested a viable direction should you address the organization at large. You may not be able to offer a certain solution right away, but avoid presenting the group with nothing better than a dead end.

LESSON 15
LEADERSHIP IS ABOUT EVERYONE ELSE

"After the assault on Blair House I learned that the men who want to keep me alive are the ones who get hurt and not the president."

—Diary entry, February 20, 1952

Harry Truman mightily resented the way the November 1, 1950, attempt on his life cramped his style. (For the story, see "Live What You Believe" in Chapter 5.) Accustomed to walking the streets of the capital at the brisk military stride of 120 steps per minute, Truman observed in his February 20, 1952, diary entry:

> Since the assault on the police and the secret service, I ride across the street in a car the roof of which will turn a grenade, the windows and sides turn a bullet, and the floor will stop a land mine! Behind me in an open car ride six or seven men with automatics and machine guns. The uniformed police stop traffic in every direction—and I cross the street in state and wonder why anyone would want to live like that.

There is a rueful note in this entry but not a hint of selfishness. Truman does not begin, "Since the attempt on my life," but, "Since the assault on the police and the secret service. . . ." He was mindful that two officers were wounded and one killed in that attack. ("The people who really got hurt were wonderful

men," Truman remarked to Secretary of State Dean Acheson.)
He continued his diary entry:

> [All this fuss and protection] is a hell of a way to live.
> But after the assault on Blair House I learned that the
> men who want to keep me alive are the ones who get
> hurt and not the president. I'd always thought that I
> might be able to take care of an assassin as old Andy
> Jackson did [he lashed out at an assailant with his
> walking stick] but I found that the guards get hurt and
> not the president. So now I conform to rules without
> protest. . . .

Leadership is not a matter of self-elevation, but of elevation to
selflessness. In essence, leadership is about everyone else.

LESSON 16
PASS THE BATON

"I am extremely sorry that you have allowed a bunch of screwballs to come between us."

—Letter to Dwight D. Eisenhower, August 16, 1952

While an effective leader must identify wholeheartedly with the enterprise, he also must separate himself from it in the interest of its continuity. This is part of the selflessness of genuine leadership, and the ability to distinguish between the self and the office is one of the key elements that separate the genuine leader from the demagogue.

In the interest of the nation and the continuity of the office of president, Truman, as his second and final term drew to a close, invited both Democratic candidate Adlai Stevenson and Republican candidate Dwight Eisenhower to come to Washington for briefings both on the current organization of the White House and on the state of the union. Stevenson eagerly accepted the invitation, but Eisenhower declined. His advisers told him that it would damage his campaign. Genuinely stunned, Truman wrote a personal letter:

Dear Ike:

I am sorry if I caused you embarrassment.

What I've always had in mind was and is a continuing foreign policy. You know that is a fact, because you had a part in outlining it.

Partisan politics should stop at the boundaries of

the United States. I am extremely sorry that you have allowed a bunch of screwballs to come between us.

You have made a bad mistake and I'm hoping it won't injure this great Republic.

There has never been one like it and I want to see it continue regardless of the man who occupies the most important position in the history of the world.

May God guide you and give you light.

From a man who has always been your friend and who always wanted to be!

Sincerely,

Harry S. Truman

LESSON 17

WHY YOU'RE SO BUSY

"I am the hired man of one hundred and fifty million people and it is a job that keeps me right busy."

—Quoted in William Hillman, *Mr. President*

"Corporate malfeasance" became a buzzword in the opening years of the twenty-first century as a host of major corporations and their leaders were exposed as outright frauds, indulging in a dazzling variety of shell games with a single common object: to report losses as profits. Employees and investors were hit hard, and so was the general economy as a nervous public rushed to take its money out of stocks. There was some cold comfort, perhaps, in seeing one executive after another take the televised "perp walk," the handcuffed journey from police vehicle to courthouse door obligatory for any alleged perpetrator of crime.

But were the executives we saw on the evening news the only perpetrators?

Naked criminal fraud was not the only blow to investor confidence at the start of the new century. Investors began taking a hard look at where their money was going, and in many cases they discovered that CEOs and other corporate leaders were taking salaries and other forms of "compensation" that would have given old King Croesus reason to blush. Worse, much of this could hardly be rationalized as a reward for exceptional performance. The heads of some of the most lackluster companies received some of the most dazzling packages. Indeed, just as prenuptial agreements have become de rigueur in high-stakes marriages, so are golden parachutes the norm for high-rolling top executives. Think of a big corporation as a giant airliner, then consider that the only parachute on board belongs to the pilot.

All attempts at rationalization notwithstanding, the conclusion was inescapable: Too many business leaders were in business for themselves.

Harry Truman understood that no true leader can be in business for himself. He liked to quote James K. Polk, the more or less obscure eleventh president of the United States, whom he greatly admired. Approaching the end of his term and having chosen not to run again, Polk remarked, "I will soon cease to be a servant and will become a sovereign." A leader is the "hired man" (or woman) of the people he or she leads.

In climbing the corporate ladder, we speak of acquiring power. But it is just as true that in acquiring power, you have to sacrifice the sovereignty of the private person, the man or woman who truly—and properly—is in business only for him- or herself.

LESSON 18

ALWAYS MOVE TOWARD THE GOAL

"If each side is willing to make the thing work, it can be done, in spite of the details."

—Speech at Columbia University, April 28, 1959

A student attending the former president's Columbia University lecture program asked Truman if he thought the United States would resolve its objections to aspects of the World Court Charter and agree to abide by international adjudication and arbitration procedures as an alternative to the use of arms. Truman replied that "minor details" should not "stand in the way of preventing another war in the world." He believed that "if each side is willing to make the thing work, it can be done, in spite of the details."

One key leadership function is to maintain the group's focus on worthwhile objectives. This often requires discriminating between major and minor obstacles on the way to the chosen goal, and sometimes it even requires weighing some of those obstacles against the objective. A cool head and balanced judgment are required to prevent details from obscuring the big picture and to ensure that obstacles and detours do not bar passage to objectives that bring real benefit. See details for what they are. Overcome challenges. Resolve differences. Keep moving toward each worthwhile goal.

CHAPTER 3

RIDE THE TIGER

LESSON 19
REFUSE TO BE INTIMIDATED

"Went to bed, went to sleep, and did not worry any more."

—Diary entry, April 12, 1945, the evening after taking
the oath of office on the death of President Roosevelt

The scene is famous. At the White House and his first meeting
with reporters the day after he was sworn in as president of a nation still in the throes of a desperate war, its beloved four-term
leader suddenly dead of a cerebral hemorrhage, Truman gathered
the reporters around him.

> Boys, if you ever pray, pray for me now. I don't know
> whether you fellows ever had a load of hay fall on you,
> but when they told me yesterday what had happened,
> I felt like the moon, the stars, and all the planets had
> fallen on me.

It was the kind of moment of utterly disarming, plainspoken
honesty that would mark the Truman presidency. And yet, frank
as the statement was, it was also misleading. Truman must have
felt overwhelmed. Who wouldn't? Not only did he have to take
up the reins of a government at war, but he had to assume them
from the most universally revered American leader since George
Washington. Worst of all, FDR had rarely spoken with his vice
president, let alone formally briefed or confided in him. Truman
took office a man in the dark.

Nevertheless, his behavior when he was told of FDR's death was anything but that of a man buried under the weight of the moon, stars, and planets.

Truman was in the office of Speaker of the House Sam Rayburn, about to enjoy a drink with the Speaker and others, when Rayburn told him that Steve Early, the White House press secretary, had phoned and wanted Truman to "call him right away." Truman returned the call, and Early asked him to come to the White House "quickly and . . . quietly."

"I ran all the way," Truman later recalled. Two ushers escorted him to an elevator and the president's private quarters, where Eleanor Roosevelt was in her sitting room. It was she who said, "Harry, the President is dead."

Truman's first words, when he could find them, were supremely telling of his character: "Is there anything I can do for you?"

"Is there anything *we* can do for *you*?" Mrs. Roosevelt replied. "For you are the one in trouble now."

That was at 5:25 in the afternoon. Less than two hours later, at 7:09, Harry Truman took the oath of office from Chief Justice Harlan Stone. All present remarked on how, at the conclusion of the ceremony, he took in both hands the Bible on which he had sworn and pressed it to his lips.

He spoke briefly to the Cabinet, asking for their advice, expressing his hope that all would stay on the job, explaining that he fully anticipated they would disagree with him from time to time, but closing with the remark that all final decisions would be his and his alone and that he expected their full support once those decisions were made. The Cabinet was dismissed, only Secretary of War Henry Stimson briefly remaining behind to tell the new president that they needed to speak very soon about a "new explosive" of unimaginable power. FDR had never even told Truman about the atomic bomb.

Overwhelmed? The word is too pale to describe what Harry Truman had every right and reason to feel. Yet whatever he felt, he refused to be intimidated by the office that was, as of 7:09 P.M., his.

"Went to bed, went to sleep, and did not worry any more," he wrote in his diary. Then he woke to begin governing the nation.

LESSON 20
ACCEPT REALITY

"I decided the best thing to do was to go home and get as much rest as possible and face the music."

—Diary entry, April 12, 1945

"I was very much shocked," Harry Truman wrote in his diary the evening after he took the oath of office following the death of FDR. "I am not easily shocked but was certainly shocked when I was told of the President's death and the weight of the Government had fallen on my shoulders. I did not know what reaction the country would have to the death of a man whom they all practically worshipped. I was worried about the reaction of the Armed Forces. I did not know what effect the situation would have on the war effort, price control, war production and everything that entered into the emergency that then existed. I knew the President had a great many meetings with Churchill and Stalin. I was not familiar with any of these things and it was really something to think about but I decided the best thing to do was to go home and get as much rest as possible and face the music."

Franklin Delano Roosevelt was a great president, but he had taken no time to bring his vice president into the loop. It is doubtful that any vice president ascended to the presidency with less preparation than Harry Truman, and no one was more aware of this than Truman himself.

The well-worn Chinese saying "A journey of a thousand miles

begins with a single step" may be paraphrased for anyone who accepts the responsibility of guiding others in any enterprise: *Leadership begins by accepting reality.* It is a first step as simple as it may be profound or, under some circumstances, even profoundly terrifying.

After that first step, what next? The next step . . . and the next. Having accepted reality, honestly assess your position within it. If you lack preparation, then prepare. Do the hard work of catching up. Do not fight the problems that confront you. Work with them. Work through them. Work them out. And bear in mind the operative word: *work.*

LESSON 21
DEMOCRACY ENDS HERE

"That is the way I intend to run this."

—Notation on White House appointment sheet,
May 18, 1945, concerning a Cabinet meeting early
in Truman's first term

"I told the Cabinet members a story about President Lincoln—when he was discussing the [Emancipation] proclamation—every member of his Cabinet opposed to him making proclamation—he put the question up to the whole Cabinet and they voted No—that is very well, the President voted Yes—that is the way I intend to run this."

A leader of any organization must decide where democracy ends. He or she can and must make that decision. In the case of his Cabinet, Truman wanted a group of advisers who would feel free to argue against him whenever they thought necessary, but who would also accept the decidedly undemocratic proposition that the single vote of the president outweighed all of theirs combined.

It is important to invite free and creative thought. It is important to give your staff the message that you value their ideas and judgment. But it is equally important that they understand and accept the finality of your authority, including the authority to act, when you deem appropriate, contrary to what they suggest.

LESSON 22
MAINTAIN PERSPECTIVE

"Nearly every crisis seems to be the worst one but after it's over it isn't so bad."

—Letter to his mother, August 12, 1945

Thrust into the presidency by the sudden death of FDR in the midst of the greatest, most complex, and most destructive war in the history of humankind, Harry Truman had a right to feel overwhelmed, but he was well aware that he had no right to indulge that feeling. Whatever emotions he experienced, Truman immediately immersed himself in the situation that was now his and quickly mastered circumstances as well as feelings.

For Truman, the presidency soon became an exercise in perspective, as he wrote to his mother: "Nearly every crisis seems to be the worst one but after it's over it isn't so bad." In a high-pressure, high-stakes leadership environment, maintaining perspective geared to the continual movement of events is critically important. In other words, roll with the punches, accepting none as a knockout blow. Defeat requires surrender, and that should not be an option. Events keep moving ahead, and so should you.

LESSON 23
THE (LIMITED) VALUE OF CONTINUITY

"Every President must have a Cabinet of his own choosing. But in time of national emergency continuity of government is of paramount importance."

—*Memoirs, Volume One: Year of Decisions*

At his first meeting with the Roosevelt Cabinet, immediately after he was sworn in following the death of FDR, Truman asked all the members to stay on. The president's passing had been sudden and shocking enough, and in this time of war Truman believed it important to preserve a significant measure of continuity, which not only would reassure the people and the military, but would help his "administration to maintain existing contacts with Congress." Moreover, Truman was well aware that he "needed time to familiarize [himself] with all the urgent business confronting the government." However, even at this point he knew that "eventually there had to be changes."

Some leaders who are new to the job rush to place their stamp on the organization by making a sharp and thorough break with the past. Others are fearful of rocking the boat and introduce as few changes as possible. Blindly adhered to, neither of these extremes is an effective leadership strategy. Continuity in any organization has value and is not to be disrupted lightly, but it is a mistake to make a deity out of the status quo. Effective leaders decide on who and what they need to administer the organization, and they assemble their inner circle accordingly. Since needs as well as awareness of needs evolve, the process of creating a "new" administration may take some time, and time may also prove the continued value of some staff inherited from predecessors. Be patient and give the leadership circle sufficient time in which to evolve.

LESSON 24
HOW TO HANDLE AN ULTIMATUM

"'All right,' I replied, 'if that is the way you feel, I'll accept your resignation right now.' And I did."

—*Memoirs, Volume One: Year of Decisions*

Henry Morgenthau, Jr., the secretary of the treasury Truman inherited from the Roosevelt administration, had created an economic plan—named for him—pursuant to a meeting among Franklin Roosevelt, Winston Churchill, and Canadian prime minister Mackenzie King, that called for the postwar elimination of Germany's industrial potential in order to make that nation strictly a pastoral and agricultural community. In one of his boldest breaks with the Roosevelt program, Truman rejected the Morgenthau Plan, believing that it would devastate Germany economically and humiliate it politically, thereby repeating the terrible error of the Treaty of Versailles, which had ended World War I and so severely punished Germany that it created conditions conducive to the rise of Hitler and made a *second* world war virtually inevitable.

As Truman prepared for the July 1945 Potsdam Conference, in which he would confer with Churchill and Stalin in an effort to map out the future of the postwar world, Morgenthau asked to accompany the president to the conference. Truman had no intention of bringing along the champion and namesake of the Morgenthau Plan, and he told the secretary that he was needed more in the United States than in Potsdam. Morgenthau "replied that it was necessary for him to go and that if he could not he would have to quit."

Confronted by an ultimatum, many of us leap to one of two responses: an angry outburst or a lavish effort to smooth things over with some (usually less than satisfactory) compromise. Truman, however, accepted the terms of the ultimatum and turned them back on Morgenthau: "All right, if that is the way you feel, I'll accept your resignation right now." Morgenthau resigned, and "that was the end of the conversation and the end of the Morgenthau Plan."

The thrust of an ultimatum is to diminish the power to lead. An ultimatum is a strong-arm effort to compel a decision, and no decision made under duress can be truly the product of leadership. It is, rather, a surrender of the authority to decide.

Always look for ways either to reject the ultimatum or to turn it to your advantage. In the case of Morgenthau's ultimatum to Truman, the president used it to purge his Cabinet of a discordant voice and what he believed was a destructive economic plan. An ultimatum is an attempt to paint you into a corner. Be aware, however, that this usually requires the issuer of the ultimatum to limit his options as severely as yours. As a negotiating move, an ultimatum is a gambit, which may readily be turned against the person who risks it.

But what if, for all his dislike of the Morgenthau Plan, Truman had decided that he needed to reject the plan but retain Morgenthau? In that case, he would have avoided calling the secretary's bluff and instead would have looked for a way to let Morgenthau out of the blind alley of his own making. When someone invites you to sit on the horns of a dilemma, turn the invitation back on him. Invite *him* to formulate a third-course alternative to the either/or proposition on the table. Present *him* with ownership of the problem he has made for you. In this way, you do not relinquish leadership, yet you both challenge and empower the other person.

LESSON 25
ORGANIZE FOR ACTION

"I wanted to establish governmental lines so clearly that I would be able to put my finger on the people directly responsible in every situation."

—*Memoirs, Volume One: Year of Decisions*

Harry Truman's admiration for his predecessor was vast, but it was not unbounded. He believed FDR had been a great executive but a poor administrator, who left the executive branch inefficiently organized. "There was too much duplication of functions," Truman complained, "too much 'passing of the buck,' and too much confusion and waste." He understood that many of the problems were "inevitable as the war kept piling additional burdens on the government," but Truman was determined to reorganize the executive branch in order "to establish governmental lines so clearly that I would be able to put my finger on the people directly responsible in every situation."

Truman immediately set about securing from Congress the authority to make the necessary changes, which included radically reorganizing the White House apparatus and streamlining communication with the other branches of government. Truman also set into motion the creation of a Cabinet-level Department of Welfare, and, most difficult and critical of all, he surrounded himself "with assistants and associates who would not overstep the bounds of . . . delegated authority" and who "were people I could trust."

Some leaders build their organizations from scratch; others inherit their office. In both cases, however, ample room should be made for creativity and innovation. There is no good reason to build or to accept an administrative structure that functions inefficiently. The objective should be to organize for productive action, not to flounder among bureaucratic mazes and barricades intended to promote and preserve inaction. Physicists and engineers understand that no machine is 100 percent efficient. Even the finest automobile engine transforms only a fraction of the energy that drives it into useful motion that propels the car. However, this does not alter the goal of designing engines that usefully transform as much energy as possible. Like machines, organizations suffer in varying degrees from the effects of entropy, an inevitable loss of useful energy. Accept the fact of entropy, but never give up guiding your organization to minimize its effects.

LESSON 26
CLAIM YOUR TURF

"The State Department doesn't have a policy unless I support it."

—Press conference, January 31, 1946

A coup d'état is a sudden, often violent seizure of authority from the designated leader. But it doesn't take a coup d'état to reduce a leader's clout. Far more common than the dramatic coup is the erosion of authority so gradual that it may go unnoticed until the leader is leader in name only or, perhaps, not even that. Power and authority must be defended vigilantly, not so much against big moves—you generally see those coming—but against a subtle chipping away.

"Mr. President," a reporter began during a presidential press conference, "do you support the State Department's policy that the United States should . . ." And Truman stopped him dead: "The State Department doesn't have a policy unless I support it."

If you fail to define yourself, others will define you—and rarely to your benefit. Truman's statement preempted such an unwelcome definition. He correctly and wisely rejected it, not even allowing the proposition to be completed.

LESSON 27
REJECT ANXIETY

"I've been shot at by experts. . . ."

—Letter to his cousin Ethel Noland, November 17, 1950

"Live What You Believe," a lesson in Chapter 5, details the attempted assassination of Harry S. Truman by two Puerto Rican nationalists on November 1, 1950. Concerning the event, Truman reported in a letter to his cousin Ethel Noland that "I was the only calm one in the house. You see I've been shot at by experts and unless your name's on the bullet you needn't be afraid—and that of course you won't find out, so why worry."

This might be dismissed as bravado, and bravado it may in fact have been—but it worked for Truman, who had lived through the thick of World War I. Fear is natural, normal, and, often, useful. It may keep us from doing something foolish. It may prevent unnecessary exposure to danger. It may save lives. But there is a point at which fear becomes chronic, and that emotion—anxiety—is destructive.

At the very least, anxiety wastes energy, discourages creative risk, and even erodes health. At worst, it creates out-and-out paralysis. Truman found a way around anxiety by accepting the physical risks that go with being president and by adopting a certain fatalism about them. A degree of danger, he recognized, was part of his job, and either he could be perpetually anxious about it or he could accept it, work around and in spite of it, and give up worrying about it.

This embrace of bravado only went so far. It ended where genuine good judgment was called for. As he explained later in his letter to Ethel Noland: "I hope it won't happen again. They [the Secret Service] won't let me go walking or even cross the street on foot. I say 'they' won't, but it causes them so much anguish that I conform—a hard thing for a Truman to do as you know, particularly when he could force them to do as he wants. But I want no more guards killed. . . ." For Truman, the bravado ended where consideration for the welfare of others began.

LESSON 28
FIRST, BE SURE YOU WANT IT

"Being president is sort of a working job. . . ."
—Letter to his cousin Nellie Noland, November 25, 1952

Harry Truman had little affection for his successor, Dwight David Eisenhower, who rudely rebuffed his advice and his offers of help with the transition of leadership. Truman believed Eisenhower had been a great general, but, once out of uniform, Ike proved to be "a dumb son of a bitch." What Truman most objected to was what he perceived as Eisenhower's laziness. Writing to his cousin Nellie Noland about a November 18, 1952, transition-related meeting with the president-elect, Truman rather gleefully observed: "Ike came to see me and he was not at all happy when he left. He found that being president is sort of a working job and Ike doesn't like to work—either mentally or physically. What a fool he is to have left 'social security' in the form of lifetime pay and emoluments of a 5-star general and move into the most controversial and nerve-wracking job in the world!"

"Uneasy lies the head that wears a crown," Shakespeare wrote, or as one of the great crown wearers, Queen Elizabeth I, put it in her famed "Golden Speech" to Parliament in 1601, "To be a king and wear a crown is a thing more glorious to them that see it than it is pleasant to them that bear it." Many aspiring leaders find such sentiments as hard to believe as the old saw about money not buying happiness, but those who actually have money or hold leadership positions are almost always thoroughly persuaded. Before you envy the king, look beyond the glitter of the crown and ponder its heft.

Important note concerning leadership: First, be sure you want it.

LESSON 29
EXERCISE THE MIND, EXERCISE THE BODY

"I walk and swim and worry very little. I appoint people in responsible positions to worry for me. You have no idea how satisfactory that policy is."

—Quoted in William Hillman, *Mr. President*

In his 1980 *Aspects of the Presidency*, John Hersey repeated something Truman said, one way or another, many times: "You can't be mentally fit unless you're physically fit." This was hardly a radical idea in the 1940s and 1950s, but relatively few executives and leaders worried much back then about getting up from behind their desks. Today, many upper-level managers make time for exercise, and companies may provide fitness-club memberships or even maintain on-site gyms.

If Truman acknowledged the mind-body connection, he also understood that it ran both ways. You couldn't be mentally fit without being physically fit, and you couldn't be physically fit if worry had rendered you mentally unfit.

While many of us find it difficult to begin and maintain a regimen of physical fitness, even more of us have a hard time giving up worry. It's easy to understand inertia where exercise is concerned, but why do so many people have such a hard time not worrying? Worry is proof that we care deeply about something, and at some level of consciousness many of us believe that demonstrating concern through worry will somehow bring about a satisfactory resolution to whatever problem or issue troubles us.

This is magical thinking, a belief that a state of thought or feeling will create a desired outcome in the world.

Of course, the fact is that worrying works no magic. If anything, it imperils the desired outcome. A salesperson worried about making a sale unintentionally communicates all of her doubts to her prospect and thereby stacks the odds against closing. Even more serious, as Truman well understood, is the harm chronic worry does to the human constitution. Stress kills. In his 1996 memoir, *Balance of Power: Presidents and Congress from the Era of McCarthy to the Age of Gingrich*, former Speaker of the House Jim Wright characterized the presidency as a "man-killing job" and recalled that a prominent physician observed that four years in the White House aged a person at least fifteen. Truman, who confessed to working eighteen hours a day seven days a week, emerged in 1953 from almost eight years in the White House a vigorous man of sixty-eight who would live an active retirement until his death, at age eighty-eight, in 1972.

LESSON 30
NO EASY WAY

"I do not know of any easy way to be President."

—*Memoirs, Volume Two: Years of Trial and Hope*

Perhaps the single most useful lesson the career of Harry S. Truman teaches is that leadership, done right, done with one's whole heart and mind, is not easy. Why is this useful to know? Because knowing that leadership is hard work may help explain why you are so tired at the end of the day. If leadership takes an awful lot out of you, it's not because you're doing it wrong. Quite the contrary. Hard work is the work of a leader.

LESSON 31
CHOOSE TO RIDE

"Being a president is like riding a tiger. A man has to keep on riding or be swallowed."

—Speech at Columbia University, April 27, 1959

Picture the top person in any organization. He or she sits in a comfortable chair behind a costly desk. That snapshot image is probably universal. Asked to picture the big boss, this is the picture we see. What's wrong with this picture? Everything.

In any high-stakes enterprise, the leader, whatever her office decor, is not cozily ensconced in a chair behind a desk but, rather, perches precariously on a tiger. Leadership is a dynamic exercise, not a steady state. Allow yourself to become complacent, and the enterprise you lead will consume you.

Your only viable choice as a leader is to ride, to stay with the beast, to master and direct it. This is a choice that must be made continually, for there are innumerable temptations to quit and sit back. Others, some meaning well, some with different motives, will invite you to relinquish the reins, if only for a little while. Circumstances at a given moment may invite relaxation. But there is no safe way to dismount from a tiger—of that all leaders may be assured.

LESSON 32
CONFLICT CAN BE GOOD

"Now there's been a great deal of conversation about the constitutional set-up, and it sometimes causes strained relations between the President and the Congress and the courts. Well, it was set up that way on purpose."

—Speech at Columbia University, April 27, 1959

Most managers and leaders avoid conflict or, at the very least, seek and hope to avoid it. Truman understood that such a leadership strategy was not only impossible for the person in the White House, it was undesirable, because it ran contrary to the way the system was set up. Conflict—checks and balances—is built into American government, as Truman explained to his Columbia University audience, "so that no man-on-horseback could take charge, so that no man could become a dictator."

Most of us would agree that a system of checks and balances is a good thing in democratic government, but is built-in conflict a positive force in a business organization?

The answer is: sometimes.

Some organizations thrive on harmony and are either grateful for that blissful state or take it so much for granted that they are blissfully ignorant of their good fortune. It is also true that some organizations are destroyed by conflict at various levels. Yet conflict can also be the engine that drives the enterprise forward. Some leaders are directors who virtually single-handedly determine the course taken by the group. Others, however, work best in a climate of dialogue or debate. They need to bounce their ideas off others and wrestle with others over direction, objective, and means. For these leaders, the universe is decidedly Newtonian: Every action has an equal and opposite reaction. In some organizations, such contrary movements cancel each other out, with destructive results. In others, however, the result is enhanced forward thrust.

A leader should not automatically embrace organizational harmony or fear organizational conflict. When harmony oozes into stagnation, consider introducing a little conflict into the organization. Confronted by conflict, resist knee-jerk impulses to suppress it. Instead, make the best of it. Exploit it. An explosion may be just what the organization needs.

LESSON 33
IGNORING A PROBLEM IS NOT
SOLVING A PROBLEM

"Nonaction was characteristic of Eisenhower as president because he proved to be such a dumb son of a bitch when he got out of his uniform. . . ."

—Quoted in *Where the Buck Stops: The Personal and Private Writings of Harry S. Truman* (Margaret Truman, ed.)

Harry Truman entrusted to the care of his daughter, Margaret, a large number of papers, which he hoped she would shape into a book *after* both he and his wife were dead. As frank as "Give 'em Hell Harry" was in life, he kept some sentiments to himself until he had gone to his grave. Truman never made any secret of his dislike for his successor, Dwight Eisenhower (see Lesson 28), but only in the posthumous *Where the Buck Stops* did the full extent of his disdain find expression.

In a chapter titled "Why I Don't Like Ike" he recalled being interviewed by "a young fellow who was putting together a television show, and he asked me what I thought about Eisenhower's nonaction on Castro." Truman replied that, by ignoring Castro, Eisenhower had sacrificed an opportunity "to get him on our side rather than Russia's." Truman told the interviewer that, had he still been president,

> when Castro started that revolution against Batista and won, I'd have picked up the phone and made friends with him, offered him financial aid and other

kinds of help in getting Cuba on its feet. I don't think for a minute that Castro was a locked-in pro-Russian at that point; I think he turned toward Russia because when he looked at us, all he could see was a bunch of backs turned away from him. I'd have said, "Listen, Fidel, come on down here to Washington and let's talk." Maybe I'd have hinted that it would be nice if he took a haircut and a good shower before he came, but speaking seriously, I'd have seen to it that we had a sensible meeting and worked things out. . . .

Eisenhower, however, just sat "on his behind and hope[d] that if he didn't seem to notice Castro and the other Cuban revolution-aries, they might go away. . . ."

Ignoring a problem does not solve a problem. Instead of avoiding problems, engage them, and do so sooner rather than later. As Truman noted, Eisenhower sat on his behind, but "the Russians didn't sit on their behind and they got Castro nice and deep in their pockets." The failure to face and resolve a problem does not merely leave the problem unresolved; in a complex and competitive environment, inaction often turns *your* problem into *someone else's* opportunity.

LESSON 34
STAND AGAINST THE DEMAGOGUES

"I want to warn you, though, that sometime or another you will have experience with demagogues and with hysteria, just as I have, and you have got to stand fast, because when those things take place, the demagogues try to find a goat on whom they can operate."

—Seminar on Statecraft, Columbia University,
April 28, 1959

Demagogues are a danger in any organization. They seek power by appealing to the least productive or even the most destructive aspects of popular sentiment. Truman was all too familiar with the leading demagogue of early 1950s America, Senator Joseph McCarthy of Wisconsin, who whipped many Americans into hysteria over alleged widespread infiltration of U.S. government and institutions by Communist sympathizers and Soviet spies.

The creation and exploitation of hysteria is the modus operandi of the demagogue, and this holds as true in a business organization as it does in government. From a variety of motives, individuals within the organization become poison pills who disseminate rumor and gossip, raise unfounded doubts, and generally undermine legitimate leadership.

Demagogues must be dealt with. It is a grave mistake, however, to attempt to defeat them with more demagoguery—that is, by pandering to the group. Demagoguery is the antithesis of leadership, because it feeds off the needs and insecurities of the

group. Demagoguery follows rather than leads; the antidote is
leadership. Address the demagogue's issues, trace the hysteria to
its roots, then seize the initiative from the demagogue by commu-
nicating with the organization. Share the relevant facts of the
matter at issue, identify problems, then present solutions. Engage
the group in the execution of these solutions. Invite advice and
other input you deem useful, but be certain that in the end, you
are the one who issues unambiguous instructions. A demagogue
mouths the fears of the group. A leader turns from fear to facts,
frankly shares information, defines difficulties, presents solutions,
engages the group, but always gives the final orders.

LESSON 35

SYMPATHY

"The best thing to do is to let him alone."

—Letter to Pierce Adams, August 14, 1963

A Mr. Pierce Adams wrote to the retired president suggesting that he send a letter to the owner of the Kansas City baseball team complaining about "their lack of winning." Truman thanked Adams for the letter, but declined to accept the suggestion:

> I can't go along with you on that sort of approach for the simple reason that when I was President, every Tom, Dick and Harry tried to tell me what to do.
>
> The President of the baseball team knows what to do and the best thing to do is to let him alone.

This was a response born of experience, a gesture of sympathetic understanding from one leader concerning another. Unfortunately, few people can resist an invitation to criticize the powers that be, and for any leader to expect that he or she will be left alone to lead is wishful thinking. A leader gets all sorts of input—advice and criticism, solicited as well as unsolicited, and even some praise. *Listen* to it all, but understand that in the end, you must truly *hear* your own voice above all others.

LESSON 36
ABANDON PESSIMISM

"I have never seen pessimists make anything work, or contribute anything of lasting value."

—Quoted in David S. Thomson,
HST: A Pictorial Biography

It is easy to confuse pessimism with realism. Pessimists believe the two are synonymous, but in truth, pessimism is a philosophical shell. A defense against the possibility of failure, pessimism is a defense against possibility, period. It engenders not prudence or caution but inertia, and it is inertia that so frequently proves the pessimist right. In the absence of action, things often *do* decay and fall apart. Certainly, by definition, inaction results in the failure of fulfillment of expectations.

You cannot afford the disastrous comfort of pessimism. But consider this: An enterprise in which no cause for optimism can be found is not worth leading. Just make certain that you've looked very hard and absolutely everywhere before you write off the feasibility of hope.

LESSON 37
BUT THEY WEREN'T ELECTED

"There are probably hundreds of people better qualified than I am to be president, but they weren't elected."

—Quoted in David S. Thomson,
HST: A Pictorial Biography

You can spend years and a fortune on psychoanalysis in an effort to overcome your self-doubts, but it is quicker and cheaper simply to accept those feelings and work with, around, and in spite of them. Are you good enough? Are you up to the task? Is someone better? The answers to these and similar questions are, in a word, irrelevant. All that matters is that you are the leader. This is the only reality that counts, and you must act solely within this reality, as Harry S. Truman did.

LESSON 38
PRACTICE PRAGMATISM

"The thing a president has to do in order to meet a situation, in my view, is to read the law, read the Constitutional background for that law, and make up his mind what he wants to do and tell the lawyers what he wants to do and have them find a legal way to do it. And if they don't, do it anyhow, and then they'll find the legal way."

—Quoted in *Where the Buck Stops: The Personal and Private Writings of Harry S. Truman* (Margaret Truman, ed.)

The Roman philosopher Publilius Syrus observed, "Necessity knows no law." Truman understood that a leader must often walk a fine line between necessity and law, but in the end, he came down on the side of necessity. This is the essence of pragmatic leadership.

The pragmatic leader looks for a way to reconcile necessary action with existing rules and accepted practices. Absent this, however, action takes precedence over the status quo, which may then be modified after the fact and in the fullness of time.

LESSON 39
LEADERSHIP IS NO ACCIDENT

"Most men don't aspire to the presidency. It comes to them by accident."

—Quoted in *Where the Buck Stops: The Personal and Private Writings of Harry S. Truman* (Margaret Truman, ed.)

A legendary political campaigner, Truman nevertheless attached less importance to the fact of being elected than to performance once in office. Nor was there any guarantee that the better leader would always be the chosen candidate. Defeat, Truman wrote, is "a preference for somebody else for that particular office at that particular moment, that's all."

If election to office is very nearly an "accident," leadership is not. Once in a position of responsibility—no matter how that position was attained—the candidate must transform himself or herself into a leader through policy, judgment, and action. Too many presidents, as Truman saw it, achieved election without ever achieving leadership. Presidents Taylor, Fillmore, Pierce, Buchanan, Grant, Harding, Coolidge, and Truman's own successor, Dwight David Eisenhower, all held office but failed to lead once they attained it.

CHAPTER 4

UNSTUFF A STUFFED SHIRT

LESSON 40
KNOW A HYPOCRITE
WHEN YOU SEE ONE

"Early in the morning . . . , the good church members and Anti-Saloon Leaguers would come in for their early-morning drink behind the prescription case at ten cents an ounce. They would wipe their mouths, peep through the observation hole in the front of the case, and depart. This procedure gave a fourteen-year-old boy quite a viewpoint on the public front of leading citizens and 'amen-corner-praying' churchmen."

—*Memoirs, Volume One: Year of Decisions*

At age fourteen, Harry Truman took an early-morning job opening and tidying up a neighborhood drugstore in his hometown of Independence. In those days, pharmacies regularly stocked liquor "for medicinal purposes," and young Harry was clearly fascinated by the spectacle of those who publicly preached against drink and advocated temperance furtively buying a drink first thing in the morning. For Truman, it was an indelible lesson in hypocrisy. "There were saloons aplenty around the square in Independence, and many leading men in town made no bones about going into them and buying a drink. I learned to think more highly of them than I did of the prescription-counter drinkers."

The message of the fairy tale about the emperor's new clothes is that pretension and hypocrisy, while common, are easily seen through—even by a child. At fourteen, Harry Truman knew a hypocrite when he saw one. As adults, we should know at least as much and, even more, have the courage to reject the complacency that accepts hypocrisy as a social norm.

LESSON 41

MANAGE YOUR PRIMA DONNAS

"It is a very great pity we have to have stuffed Shirts . . . in key positions."

—Diary entry, June 17, 1945

Like several other presidents, Truman had a "kitchen cabinet," a trusted group of informal advisers, in addition to the officially appointed Cabinet. On June 17, 1945, he conferred with his kitchen cabinet on the presidential yacht *Sequoia* and discussed, among other things, "what to do with Mr. Prima Donna, Brass Hat, Five Star MacArthur. He's worse than the Cabots and the Lodges—they at least talked with one another before they told God what to do. Mac tells God right off. It is a very great pity we have to have stuffed Shirts like that in key positions." When the Japanese attacked the Philippines at the beginning of the war in the Pacific, FDR ordered the evacuation of General Douglas MacArthur, leaving his subordinate, Lieutenant General Jonathan Wainwright, behind to defend the islands as best he could. The result was a defense as heroic as it was hopeless, and Wainwright and his men spent the rest of the war under inhuman confinement as prisoners of the Japanese. Truman continued his diary entry: "I don't see why in Hell Roosevelt didn't order Wainwright home and let MacArthur be a martyr! . . . We'd [have] had a real General and a fighting man if we had Wainwright and not a play actor and a bunco man such as we have now."

It is no secret that Truman distrusted and disliked Douglas MacArthur. As leaders, they were diametric opposites. William Manchester's classic biography of MacArthur is aptly titled *American Caesar*. Whereas MacArthur was a Caesar, Truman saw the ideal of Roman leadership not in Caesar but in Cincinnatus, the farmer appointed dictator of Rome in 458 B.C. for the purpose of rescuing a Roman consular army that was surrounded on Mount Algidus by rebels called the Aequi. Cincinnatus led a successful campaign against the Aequi, defeated them, saved Rome, and then, having done his duty, immediately renounced the dictatorship and returned quietly to his farm. As early as June 1945, while just about everyone else hailed MacArthur as an unalloyed hero, Truman recognized the potential for crisis and saw MacArthur as a management problem. The crisis would come, however, not in World War II, but in Korea, when MacArthur, as supreme commander of United Nations forces there, repeatedly defied the authority of the president and was, in Truman's word, "fired" for it (see "Authority: Don't Give It Up to a Dumb Son of a Bitch," in Chapter 6).

Truman never liked "stuffed shirts," but what was at issue in the case of MacArthur was far more than an absence of personal affection. Truman recognized that stuffed shirts posed dangers to leadership. They committed the leadership sin of putting themselves not only before and above those they led, but before and above everyone else, including those whose job it was to lead *them*. It would be best, Truman thought, to operate in an organization without stuffed shirts, but he understood that was not always possible and, accepting this reality, he resolved to work with them as far as he could. In the case of MacArthur, Truman monitored without second-guessing him. He did not let the general's tremendous popularity color his ongoing assessment of MacArthur's performance, and when that performance became unacceptable, he fired him. Truman never let the man loom larger than his deeds.

LESSON 42
KNOW YOUR LIMITS

"The people can never understand why the president does not use his supposedly great power to make 'em behave. Well all the president is, is a glorified public relations man who spends his time flattering, kissing, and kicking people to get them to do what they are supposed to do anyway."

—Letter to his sister, Mary Jane, November 14, 1947

One of the biggest mistakes a leader can make is to believe that his authority comes from his official title—president, chairman, chief, supervisor, whatever—or from his job description. These words do constitute a kind of theory of leadership, but they do not confer the actual authority of leadership. Ultimately, that authority comes from the people who allow themselves to be led. A leader earns his authority, day by day, from the other members of the enterprise.

To rely on mere words and official titles for leadership authority is to be an empty suit or a stuffed shirt. No one knew this better than Harry Truman, who understood that the president could not compel compliance. More accurately, he understood that any so-called compliance obtained under compulsion is at best mere obedience—grudging, shallow, and, therefore, of no positive and enduring value to the nation. To be worth anything, a leader must earn compliance, often through patient, humble persuasion. The leader's job is to guide members of the organization and to bring out the best of which they are capable.

LESSON 43
APPEAR AS YOU ARE

"I thought you would like to see what I look like, even if I didn't have on any clothes."

—Quoted in David McCullough, *Truman*

Truman, the hands-down underdog in the 1948 presidential campaign against Republican contender Thomas E. Dewey, launched an exuberant whistle-stop campaign in which he traveled 31,700 rail miles to give 356 speeches, usually from the rear platform of his Pullman car. When the train pulled into Missoula, Montana, very late one night, Truman was already in bed. Learning that, despite the hour, a crowd had gathered to see and hear him, the president was not about to disappoint them, nor did he intend to keep them waiting. He put on his bathrobe over his pajamas and appeared on the rear platform.

"I am sorry I had gone to bed," he apologized, "but I thought you would like to see what I look like, even if I didn't have on any clothes."

Harry Truman understood that a robe and pajamas were amply sufficient to showcase sincerity and respect. Without these two qualities, the finest of suits is empty and the most elegant of shirts is . . . stuffed.

LESSON 44
SPEAK PLAINLY

"What we are about to do here is a neighborly act. We are like a group of householders, living in the same locality, who decide to express their community of interests by entering into a formal association for their mutual self-protection."

—"Address on the Occasion of the Signing of the
North Atlantic Treaty," April 4, 1949

No postwar international agreement was more momentous than the document creating NATO, the North Atlantic Treaty Organization, and its negotiation required hammering out complex issues at the very highest levels and for the very highest stakes. Yet in his remarks on the occasion of the signing of the treaty, Truman avoided the high-flown rhetoric such ceremonies typically summon forth. Instead, he captured the significance of the event in a single vivid, homely simile that the entire world could instantly and thoroughly understand. This was very much in character for Truman; for example, in an April 11, 1951, radio address on U.S. policy in the Far East, Truman began: "I want to talk to you plainly tonight about what we are doing in Korea. . . . We are trying to prevent a third world war."

Good leadership language does not puff up or embellish. It clarifies and strips away, leaving nothing behind but sharply etched meaning.

LESSON 45
INVEST IN GRATITUDE

"You always do the right thing."

> —Letter to Secretary of State Dean Acheson,
> November 28, 1949

Whether you are president of the United States, president of a big corporation, owner of a small business, or manager of a department, it is easy to take for granted the courtesy your subordinates and co-workers offer you. Don't let this happen. Respond to respect with respect and also with thanks. A courteous exchange is in and of itself empowering. It enhances the sense of community that all organizations require. As a leader, you can amplify that enhancement.

When Secretary of State Dean Acheson took time out to pay his president a special courtesy, Truman responded to it in a special way. He made the effort to amplify it: "It was good of you to see us off," he wrote Acheson. "You always do the right thing. I'm still a farm boy and when the Secretary of State of the greatest Republic comes to the airport to see me off on a vacation, I can't help but swell up a little."

Make the most of every kind and decent act offered to you by the people with whom you work. Celebrate them. It is an investment in gratitude that pays off in a stronger, more dedicated, more focused organization. It helps transform a group of individual workers into an effective community of colleagues.

LESSON 46
JESUS IN A STUFFED SHIRT

"I've an idea if Jesus were here his sympathies would be with the thieves. . . ."

—Diary entry, June 1, 1952

In his diary, the president took note of a newspaper item: "A couple of golden crowns with all kinds of expensive jewels have been stolen from a Catholic shrine in Brooklyn. The crowns were on images of Jesus Christ and Mary his mother." He went on:

> I've an idea if Jesus were here his sympathies would be with the thieves and not with the Pharisees who crowned him with gold and jewels.
>
> The only crown he ever wore was one of thorns placed there by the emissaries of the Roman Emperor and the Jewish Priesthood. He came to help the lowly and the down trodden. But since Constantine the Great he has been taken over by the Despots of both Church and State.

On the grand scale of world history, it was once again the old story of what Truman liked to call the "stuffed shirts," the co-optation and perversion of a simple and noble purpose by those with any number of ulterior motives and self-serving agendas. Truman believed it a leader's duty to preserve—or, if necessary, to restore—the nobility of noble purposes and the direct simplicity of original objectives. He thought that a leader should champion what is right and defend it against adulteration by the stuffed shirts of the world.

It is easy and tempting to mistake the trappings of leadership for the legitimate objectives of leadership. The first years of the twenty-first century have given us many examples of executives who led their organizations to ruin, only to walk away from the wreckage with outrageous personal wealth. This is piracy, not leadership, the true reward of which is the success of the enterprise.

LESSON 47
UNSTUFF YOUR OWN SHIRT

"My choice early in life was either to be a piano player in a whorehouse or a politician. To tell the truth, there's hardly a difference."

—Quoted in Robert Alan Aurthur, "The Wit and Sass of Harry S. Truman," *Esquire*, August 1971

Throughout his long career, Harry Truman repeatedly identified himself as a politician (a "statesman," he said, "is what they call a good politician *after* he's dead"), and, as he made clear in a talk to Columbia University students in 1959, "I'm proud to be called a politician, for it's a great honor." Yet Truman was not above piercing his own balloon when it came to the profession of politics, as he did in the memorable quip quoted by a writer for *Esquire*—a magazine Truman professed to admire, until (he said) they started putting all those girls in it.

The retired president could not resist an opportunity to deflate pretension, especially his own. Self-deprecation is a pungent spice and must be used sparingly. Not only is it preferable to bland clichés and pretentious pabulum, but a joke you tell on yourself tends to rally others to your defense and support.

LESSON 48
BE MORE THAN AN EMPTY SUIT

"Of course, a wonderful appearance of a public leader is a great asset if he has something behind that public appearance to go with it."

—Quoted in *Where the Buck Stops: The Personal and Private Writings of Harry S. Truman* (Margaret Truman, ed.)

Truman was hardly a vain man, although he was always meticulous about his appearance, wore exquisitely tailored suits, and in the 1930s took some pride in having made a newspaper's list of the nation's ten best-dressed senators. At the same time, he delighted in the fashion sense of one of his favorite presidents, Thomas Jefferson, who (Truman pointed out) "didn't seem to give a damn about his clothes other than to insist that everything he wore fit loosely and comfortably, and more than once wore old clothes and house slippers."

What Truman claimed never to understand was why "some sections of the press kept referring to me as 'that little man in the White House.'" In the posthumous *Where the Buck Stops: The Personal and Private Writings of Harry S. Truman*, the president wrote that he never let himself get bothered by anything the press said about him, but then admitted, parenthetically, "Well, maybe I let it bother me a bit, but it really *is* nonsense." As proof that press characterizations of him as short were incorrect, Truman protested that he was five feet ten, compared to Coolidge and Teddy Roosevelt, both five-eight, and Ulysses S. Grant, who almost missed enrollment at West Point because the minimum height requirement was five feet. As for Ike Eisenhower, Truman pointed out that he was five-ten, just like him. Were some presidents taller? Of course. Lincoln, the tallest, was six-four and Washington six-two, but, Truman noted:

> Some of our nonentity presidents were also tall: Millard Fillmore was six feet tall, James Buchanan was about six one, and Chester A. Arthur was six feet two.
>
> Anyway, I don't think Washington's and Lincoln's commanding height had much to do with why they were respected. I think their leadership came from what was inside them. Of course, a wonderful appearance of a public leader is a great asset if he has something behind that public appearance to go with it. Otherwise, it isn't worth anything; otherwise it's just deceptive like Harding's handsomeness or Eisenhower's smile.

CHAPTER 5

SET THE BEST EXAMPLE

LESSON 49
ACTION SPEAKS LOUDER

"I didn't come over here to get along with you."

—Remarks to noncommissioned officers, Battery D, 2nd
Battalion, 129th Field Artillery, France, July 11, 1918

In that spring of 1917 when the United States entered the "Great War," World War I, Harry Truman was a farmer near Grandview, Missouri. At thirty-three, he was two years over the age limit set by the brand-new Selective Service Act. He would not have been drafted. He was not expected to serve. Not only was he overage, he was so nearsighted as to be helpless without his glasses, and, as a farmer, he was part of an industry deemed vital to the war effort.

But the thirty-three-year-old nearsighted farmer chose to enlist in the National Guard, helped organize an artillery battery, and was elected its lieutenant. Sent overseas and transferred to the regular army, he was given further artillery training, promoted to captain, and assigned to command the "wild Irish" of Battery D, 2nd Battalion, 129th Field Artillery, an outfit infamous for chewing up its commanders and spitting them out.

Approaching his first combat command for the initial assembly, Truman was terrified. "I could just see my hide on the fence," he later recalled. "Never on the front or anywhere else have I been so nervous."

Instead of haranguing the troops, Truman inspected them, silently walking up and down the ranks. When he was finished, he gave the command "Dismissed!" He turned away and began walking. The assembled men collectively issued a Bronx cheer. Truman neither stopped nor said a word. Later in the day, Battery D generally misbehaved, pretending to stampede their horses, and fighting with one another after taps. Truman did not intervene.

Early the next morning, Captain Harry S. Truman posted a list—a long list—consisting of most of the noncommissioned officers in the battery, each of whom Truman had busted in rank. He then summoned the handful of noncoms he hadn't busted.

"I didn't come over here to get along with you. You've got to get along with me. And if there are any of you who can't, speak up right now and I'll bust you right back now."

As Truman later remarked: "We got along."

But he did not stop at busting the insubordinate noncoms. As soon as their new captain took command, everyone noticed that the food got a lot better, and they soon discovered that they could talk with "Captain Harry" as they could with no other officer.

He worked tirelessly at earning the loyalty of his men. Typical was an incident in which, encountering an enlisted artilleryman who had injured his ankle, he dismounted from his horse and invited the man to ride. A colonel passing by did not like the sight of an officer on foot and an enlisted man riding. He ordered the soldier to dismount. Captain Truman stopped the soldier, turned to the colonel, and said, "You can take these bars off my shoulders, but as long as I'm in charge of this battery the man's going to stay on that horse." The colonel turned away. The soldier rode on. And Harry Truman walked with his men.

Lead by action and example; demonstrate uncompromising discipline, loyalty, and compassion.

LESSON 50
SPEAK FROM EXPERIENCE

"I know the strain, the mud, the misery, the utter weariness of the soldier in the field. And I know too his courage, his stamina, his faith in his comrades, his country, and himself."

—"Address to the Armed Forces of the United States Throughout the World," April 17, 1945

After the death of Franklin Roosevelt, President Truman was anxious to address a message to the troops, who had, he understood, lost a great leader for whom most felt deep affection. Truman did not want to offer himself as a replacement for FDR, but he did want to create a bond of solidarity with the soldiers and sailors. "*We*," he said, "have lost a hard-hitting chief and an old friend of the services. . . . *Our* hearts," he said, "are heavy." But he went on: "However, the cause which claimed Roosevelt, also claims us. He never faltered—nor will *we!*"

Having used the first person plural grammatically to identify himself with the troops, Truman went on to identify with their experience even more concretely:

> As a veteran of the first World War, I have seen death on the battlefield. When I fought in France with the 35th Division, I saw good officers and men fall, and be replaced.
>
> I know that this is also true of the officers and men

of the other services, the Navy, the Marine Corps, the Coast Guard, and the Merchant Marine.

I know the strain, the mud, the misery, the utter weariness of the soldier in the field. And I know too his courage, his stamina, his faith in his comrades, his country, and himself.

Effective leadership searches for the common points that join leader and led, management and labor, and, having identified these points, it holds them up for all to see.

LESSON 51
MEASURE YOUR TRUST

". . . because I trusted him . . ."

—Diary entry, May 22, 1945

Harry Hopkins gained national fame in the 1930s as Franklin Roosevelt's chief New Deal manager and soon became FDR's closest personal adviser and frequent emissary during World War II. Conservatives in both the Democratic and Republican parties thought Hopkins too far to the left, which made him a controversial choice when, in May 1945, President Truman sent him to Russia as his personal representative to Stalin in an attempt to shore up the deteriorating relations between the United States and its Soviet ally. To Joseph Davies, former U.S. ambassador to the Soviet Union, Truman explained (as he noted in his diary on May 22, 1945) that he'd "sent Harry Hopkins to see Stalin with instructions to tell Stalin what my views were and that I'd be pleased to meet him face to face." Why Hopkins? "Because I trusted him and because he had been Roosevelt's messenger to Russia on a previous and similar occasion" and because "he had horse sense and knew how to use it."

For Truman, personal trust, together with a de facto endorsement by FDR and his possession of a trait Truman prized above most others—"horse sense"—made Harry Hopkins the logical choice as emissary to Stalin, despite what some others might think.

Just how much did he trust Hopkins? As usual, Truman laid it all on the line. He charged Hopkins with the mission to tell Stalin "just exactly what we intended to have in the way of carrying out the agreements, purported to have been made at [the] Yalta [Conference among the allies]—that I was anxious to have a fair understanding with the Russian Government—that we never made commitments which we did not expect to carry out to the letter—we expected him to carry his agreement out to the letter and we intended to see that he did." And here, as noted on Truman's appointment sheet for May 19, 1945, was the ultimate testament of confidence: "I told Harry he could use diplomatic language, or he could use a baseball bat if he thought that was [the] proper approach to Mr. Stalin."

Trust is among a leader's most valued treasures. You need both to receive and to give trust, and when you give it, do so with scrupulous discrimination and boundless generosity—a difficult combination. The only way to avoid stinting on trust is to put your whole self into the act of trusting. Once you have decided to invest your confidence in a person, invest all the way. Truman's instructions to Hopkins were specific yet allowed for the widest possible latitude, from diplomacy to bludgeon and everything in between.

LESSON 52
FIT IN (AS MUCH AS POSSIBLE)

". . . As long as I was aboard ship I wanted to fit into the routine as much as it was possible."

—Memoirs, Volume One: Year of Decisions

In July 1945, President Truman boarded the U.S. Navy cruiser *Augusta* and set out for Europe and the conference at Potsdam, where, with Stalin and Churchill, the shape of the postwar world was to be planned. When the captain ordered a routine abandon-ship drill, the president went to his assigned station, "the No. 2 motor whaleboat on the portside of the well deck, and took part in the drill." He said that as long as he was aboard ship, he was determined to "fit into the routine as much as it was possible."

Truman "spent a good deal of time talking with the members of the crew. I also ate a meal in every mess aboard the ship, taking my place in the 'chow lines' with my aluminum tray along with the men."

At times the line you walk is a fine one between distinguishing yourself as the leader, on the one hand, and, on the other, demonstrating solidarity with those you lead. The prescription is simple: *Fit in (as much as possible)*. The execution of this principle can be tricky, however, especially if efforts to fit in are insincere or perceived as such. Truman proceeded unostentatiously. He was on a U.S. Navy ship—literally in the same boat with its crew—and he therefore respected the routines and rituals of the ship, from safety drills to meals. No more elaborate demonstration was required, and none could have been more simply effective.

LESSON 53
BE A REAL LEADER

"He stands between the next higher commander and his men."

—Letter to General Dwight D. Eisenhower,
January 16, 1946

Following the end of World War II, the United States rushed to demobilize its armed forces. General Dwight D. Eisenhower addressed Congress on the problems of demobilization, including the loss of experienced junior officers. President Truman wrote to Eisenhower to share with him his understanding of the situation. He made it clear that he fully appreciated the nature and gravity of the problem: "I know what you've been up against in this demobilization. I know you've lost your best and that the untrained and the inefficient are what we have left now." Truman presented his understanding of the importance of what might be called the "middle management" of the military: "As you know, a real leader who is a unit commander at the company level knows exactly what his men are thinking. He knows how to keep them busy in a constructive way—even if there is apparently nothing to do. He feeds them, sleeps them, and his whole life should be in their welfare."

This understanding was born of Truman's own experience as a highly respected artillery captain in World War I, and it is a good description of a "real leader," especially at the middle level of an organization: "He stands between the next higher commander and his men. He makes his non-coms responsible and if he is real makes the morale of the army."

Even at the very top, the qualities Truman described remain the stuff of *real* leadership, as the president demonstrated in his personal letter to Eisenhower. After expressing sympathetic understanding, this leader got real: "But can't we start over—from the squad up, rebuild that pride and morale which are the backbone of any organization? What can I do to help?"

Would you be a real leader? Conclude every instruction, each directive with those last six words.

LESSON 54
DON'T DO ANYTHING FOR SHOW

"I hate headline hunters and showmen as a class and individually."

—Diary entry, February 8, 1948

"I go for a walk and go to church," Truman noted in his diary on February 8, 1948.

> The preacher always treats me as a church member and not as the head of a circus. That's the reason I go to the 1st Baptist Church.
>
> One time I went to the Foundry Methodist Church, next door to the 1st Baptist, because Rev. Harris was Chaplain for the Senate when I was V.P. He made a real show of the occasion. I'll never go back. I don't go to church for show. I hate headline hunters and showmen as a class and individually.

The power and authority of sincere personal belief broadcast more widely and penetrate more deeply than any attempt to simulate such conviction, no matter how big a show is made of the simulation. There is no leadership stronger than leadership by example—provided, that is, the example is genuine.

LESSON 55
TRY SPONTANEITY

"I decided that if speaking without a prepared copy or getting away from reading a prepared text was more effective in getting my ideas and feelings across, I would use that method on the trainside talks which I planned to make in the future."

—Memoirs, Volume Two: Years of Trial and Hope

Truman's cross-country "whistle-stop" 1948 presidential campaign was celebrated for the candidate's direct, personal, spontaneous style. At each stop, Truman delivered unscripted speeches from the observation platform of the *Ferdinand Magellan*, his special Pullman car. "I was convinced," he wrote, "that the average, everyday American did not have the full story of what was going on and that it was necessary for me to get out of Washington long enough to discuss the facts of the situation directly with the people." As Truman saw it, "directly" meant in person and without even the mediation of a written script. Whereas Franklin Roosevelt's famed radio-broadcast "Fireside Chats," conversational and seemingly spontaneous, had been very carefully scripted, Truman's "trainside talks" were genuinely spontaneous, the candidate speaking to the people, as it were, in real time.

The people of the twenty-first century are intensely media-conscious. We are bathed in messages that are, in a literal sense, *mediated,* sifted through electronic technology as well as the slick sensibilities of spin doctors, press secretaries, and professional speechwriters. The result of such continual media immersion is a kind of emotional and intellectual anesthesia. People stop listening or, if they listen, they no longer hear. Against such a background, frank, direct, unscripted communication can make a powerful impact. Effective spontaneity, however, does not come easily. To communicate clearly and fully—as well as spontaneously—actually requires careful preparation. You must be thoroughly familiar with the key issues, fully informed and up to date, and you must have thought through your position on each. Armed with this preparation, it is possible to speak intelligently and persuasively from the heart and without written notes.

LESSON 56
DO AS YOU SAY

"I know I could be elected again and continue to break the old precedent as it was broken by F.D.R. It should not be done."

—Diary entry, April 16, 1950

Harry Truman did not believe a president should serve more than two terms, except in the kind of rare national emergency that presented itself in the case of Franklin Roosevelt's unprecedented four-time candidacy. In part to allow for such contingencies, he opposed passage of the Twenty-second Amendment, which placed a constitutional limit of two terms on the president, but he believed that the two-term *custom* ("custom based on the honor of the man in the office") was very important. As he wrote in his diary on April 16, 1950: "When we forget the examples of such men as Washington, Jefferson and Andrew Jackson, all of whom could have had a continuation in the office, then will we start down the road to dictatorship and ruin." Because Truman was a sitting president, the Twenty-second Amendment, ratified on February 27, 1951, did not apply to him. Moreover, he conceded that "by a quibble" he could even say he had had only a single term since he had been elected to office only once, but, as usual, he decided to discard any such evasion and instead lead by clear example: "Therefore to reestablish that [two-term] custom . . . I am not a candidate and will not accept the nomination for another term."

LESSON 57
LEARN FROM THE BEST EXAMPLES

"I spent a lot of time reading about the World's Great."

—Diary entry, January 1–2, 1952

Harry Truman was an avid reader throughout his life. He devoured histories, but he was even more passionate about biographies and autobiographies, which, he felt, presented the past more directly than any history, since the historian's business was interpretation and his Achilles' heel was bias. In a retrospective mood on New Year's Day, 1952, Truman listed the leaders he had studied as a teenager:

> Spent a lot of time reading about the World's Great. Moses, Joshua, David, Solomon, Darius I and Cyrus the Great his uncle. Alexander, Hannibal, Caesar, Antoninus Pius, Hadrian, Titus, Marcus Aurelius Antoninus, Rameses III, Cleopatra, Mark Antony, Augustus Caesar, Thothmes [Thutmose] III, Plato, Socrates, Pericles, Demosthenes, Cicero, Catos, both of them, and then Charlemagne, his father Charles Martel, Roland, John Hunyadi at Belgrade, Saladin, Suleiman the Magnificent, Jenghis Khan, Kubla Khan, Tamerlane, John Sobieski, Richelieu, Gustavus Adolphus of Sweden and Charles XII of Sweden, Alfred the Great, William of Normandy. The greatest of French Kings, Henry IV of France and King of Navarre, Francis I of

France and Charles V of Spain. Elizabeth of England and Mary of Scotland. Sir Francis Drake and Captain Kidd, Martin Luther, Frederick the Great and Maria Theresa of Austria. Wellington and Lord Russell, Disraeli, Gladstone, Washington, Jefferson, Jackson, Lincoln, Grover Cleveland, Wilson, Franklin Roosevelt and the end!

A leader's job is difficult enough without adding the reinvention of the wheel to his or her responsibilities. Learn from those who have gone before you, and in choosing your case studies, your examplars, set the bar high, preferably far above what you think you yourself can achieve. Like Truman, select your models from the "World's Great." He wrote in a memorandum of July 8, 1953: "Study the lives of great men—the truly great men. Men who have made sacrifices for the betterment of the world and their individual countries and communities."

LESSON 58
BECOME A LESSON IN ETHICS

"I would much rather be an honorable public servant and known as such than to be the richest man in the world."

—Memorandum, July 1954

"There were opportunities by the wholesale for making immense amounts of money at the county level and also in the Senate," Truman noted in a memorandum dated July 1954. But: "I lived on the salary I was legally entitled to and considered that I was employed by the taxpayers, and the people of my county, state and nation. I made no speeches for money or expenses while I was in the Senate, or as V.P. or as President."

Ethics is not merely avoiding wrongdoing. It is *doing right.* The only truly ethical course for a leader is not merely to learn or adhere to the lessons of ethical conduct, but actually to become a lesson in ethics. Model the kind of conduct you want for the entire organization. Be aware that your way of doing business is—or will soon become—the way the entire enterprise does business.

LESSON 59
THE LIFELONG APPRENTICESHIP

"I learned. . . ."

—Memorandum, July 1954

Our age is obsessed with diplomas, credentials, and formal degrees. Some cultural commentators and even a few educators have argued that we unduly prolong the adolescence of our young people by cloistering them for long years in ivory towers. To most of us, the idea of "learning on the job" seems dangerous, even irresponsible and foolhardy; yet there is no real school for leaders. If they mean to be effective, leaders have no choice, therefore, except to learn on the job. Truman's July 1954 note to himself, written perhaps in preparation for composing his memoirs, recounts his own experience of on-the-job training:

> Was elected [to the U.S. Senate] in the fall of 1934 and went to Washington in December to be sworn in as the Junior U.S. Senator from Missouri.
>
> I became a member of the Appropriations Committee, the Interstate Commerce Committee and the Public Buildings and Grounds Committee. I worked my best in all of them, carrying documents and bills home with me to work on.
>
> In Appropriations I became acquainted with every phase of the immense structure of the Federal Government. In Interstate Commerce I became familiar with

every phase of transportation. On Public Buildings and Grounds I learned about Government buildings and their upkeep.

Truman was unashamed of his lifelong apprenticeship. Few vice presidents have risen to the presidency having been furnished with less preparation by their predecessor. Undaunted, Truman did what he had done in the Senate: He learned the job, and, in the White House, he never stopped learning.

When you are put into a leadership position, the natural tendency is to present yourself as an expert, whose knowledge and judgment must by definition be superior to those of the people you are leading. The tendency may be natural, but the facts of the leadership situation are almost always contrary to it. More than anyone else in the organization, a leader must learn and keep on learning. There is no shame in it. The idea of asking a subordinate for help may seem more or less appalling, incompatible with building the organization's confidence in you, but the truth is that nothing you can ask from a subordinate is more empowering to the organization than a request for help. Learn from the members of the enterprise as you lead them.

LESSON 60
YOUR WORD

"Many drafts are usually drawn up, and this fact leads to the assumption that presidential speeches are 'ghosted.' The final version, however, is the final word of the President himself, expressing his own convictions and his policy."

—Memoirs, Volume One: Year of Decisions

Truman never tried to convey the false impression that a presidential speech was solely and spontaneously the work of the president. He explained that almost "every presidential message is a complicated business," involving many individuals and many departments of the government in order to "maintain full coordination of policy. Experts and researchers are assigned to check and compile data, because no President can or should rely entirely on his own memory." Yet while "presidential messages have to be written and rewritten many times," they "must begin with the President himself," who "must decide what he wants to say and how he wants to say it." Because many drafts are created, people may assume that a presidential speech is ghostwritten by professional speechwriters. For Truman, this conclusion was an even greater distortion than the impression that the speech was written exclusively by the president. A presidential message, Truman said, begins *and* ends with the president as his "final word."

Effective communication is vital to leadership, and there is nothing dishonest about drawing on whatever talent is available to the organization for the purpose of creating important speeches. However, no leader should ever function or be perceived as a mouthpiece for someone else's ideas and convictions. This promotes cynicism within the organization and is, in fact, an abrogation of leadership. Ensure that everything you say begins with you and, in the end, definitively represents *your* final word.

LESSON 61
LIVE WHAT YOU BELIEVE

"I've never really believed in capital punishment. I commuted the sentence of the fellow who was trying to shoot me to life imprisonment."

—Talk with Columbia University students, April 28, 1959

The White House Truman occupied showed the sad results of years of neglect. Extensive restoration work was required to make the presidential mansion fit for habitation, let alone fit to continue as a symbol of national leadership. In November 1950, while workmen gutted the interior of much of the structure, President Truman and his family lived across the street at Blair House. Unlike the White House, Blair House was separated from Pennsylvania Avenue not by a broad expanse of fenced lawn, but by nothing more than a narrow strip of grass. Thus exposed, it was a security nightmare.

Oscar Collazo and Griselio Torresola, self-styled Puerto Rican nationalists, decided that by murdering the president they could somehow win independence for their island. Shortly after 2:00 in the afternoon of November 1, 1950, the pair walked toward Blair House from opposite directions. Donald Birdzell, a White House police officer, stood guard at the bottom of the stairs leading to the front door. He heard a click, turned, and saw Collazo's Walther P-38 automatic pistol aimed at him. The weapon discharged, striking Birdzell in the leg as he reached for his own gun.

Wounded, Birdzell ran out into Pennsylvania Avenue to draw fire away from Blair House, but Collazo pushed past him, dashed up the stairs, and continued to fire, hitting Birdzell again. Two other agents, Joe Davidson and Floyd Boring, along with the twice-wounded Birdzell, opened fire from the street. Collazo was hit in the chest. In the meantime, Torresola, approaching from the other direction, shot Leslie Coffelt, a guard stationed in a sentry booth just outside the building. He also hit another guard. Mortally wounded, Coffelt returned fire, hitting Torresola in the head and killing him instantly.

Twenty-seven rounds were exchanged in the three-minute gun battle. President Truman, who had been napping, stuck his head out the window just after the last shots had been fired. He dressed quickly and rushed downstairs. After conferring with aides, he decided to continue with the appointments and activities scheduled for the day. Only later in the day, after he heard that Coffelt had died in the hospital, did Truman become visibly upset. As for himself, while out the next day on his customary walk, he dismissed the assassination attempt by telling reporters that "a President has to expect these things," but he remarked privately to Secretary of State Dean Acheson that "the people who really got hurt were wonderful men," while the gunmen had been deluded fools, "stupid as they could be."

Collazo was indicted on three charges, including the murder of Coffelt, assault with intent to kill two guards, and intent to kill the president. Found guilty of Coffelt's murder in March 1951, Collazo was sentenced to die in the electric chair on August 1, 1952. He declined his right to a clemency plea, but on July 24, 1952, days before the scheduled execution, President Truman commuted his sentence to life imprisonment.

Years later, when a Columbia University student asked the former president to talk about how a leader's personal convictions influence his policies and decisions, Truman stated that he did not believe in capital punishment. This "personal conviction" moved him to commute the death sentence of the very man who had tried to kill him. "That's the best example I can give you," Truman declared.

LESSON 62
ACTION IS THE ESSENCE
OF LEADERSHIP

"A good president must do more than just believe in what he says—he must also act on what he believes."

—Quoted in *Where the Buck Stops: The Personal and Private Writings of Harry S. Truman* (Margaret Truman, ed.)

Like many tired old sayings, *Everybody's entitled to an opinion* is perfectly true. Applied to those in leadership positions, however, it is incomplete. The essence of leadership is action. Like everyone else, leaders are entitled to their opinions. Unlike others, they are obliged to act on those opinions they deem consequential. It is not sufficient for a leader merely to express a belief. The essence of the job is to transform belief into action.

CHAPTER 6

HELL: GIVING AND GETTING

LESSON 63
MOTIVATE WITH CONSEQUENCES

"If Mr. Hillman cannot, or will not, protect the interests of the United States, I am in favor of replacing him with someone who can and will."

—Memoirs, Volume One: Year of Decisions

Motivation has become a major industry populated by high-priced speakers and "motivational consultants." Doubtless there is much to be learned from some of them. As for Harry Truman, he relied on the simplest possible motivational calculus: consequences.

As chairman of the Senate's most effective committee overseeing war-production industries, Truman saw the necessity of bringing about changes in the administration of the important Office of Production Management. In particular, the policies of Sidney Hillman, associate director of the OPM, were impeding vital production efforts. On October 29, 1941, Truman reported to the Senate that Hillman had attempted to withhold a construction contract from the low bidder because he was afraid that awarding the contract to the firm would cause labor troubles.

"A responsible company has made a low bid," Truman said to his Senate colleagues, "which it is prepared to perform and is capable of performing if not illegally interfered with. Mr. Sidney Hillman advises that it be denied the contract and that the taxpayers pay several hundred thousands of dollars more because

Mr. Hillman fears trouble from what he calls irresponsible elements in the American Federation of Labor." Truman continued: "I cannot condemn Mr. Hillman's position too strongly. First, the United States does not fear trouble from any source; and if trouble is threatened, the United States is able to protect itself. If Mr. Hillman cannot, or will not, protect the interests of the United States, I am in favor of replacing him with someone who can and will."

In motivating staff, make no idle threats and offer no intangible incentives or abstract theories. Keep motivation simple and direct by clearly setting out, on the one hand, what you expect or require and, on the other, the consequences that will *inevitably* result from either meeting those expectations and requirements or failing to do so. As Truman's remarks to the Senate demonstrate, an equation based on consequences is straightforward indeed: *If* performance is not satisfactory, *then* the responsible party will be replaced. Truman's simple formulation of the situation moved the Senate to act. Not only was Hillman removed, but the inefficient OPM was replaced by a streamlined and more powerful War Production Board, under the direction of Donald M. Nelson, an administrator who proved to be energetic and highly efficient.

LESSON 64
HAVE CONFIDENCE
IN YOUR CONVICTIONS

"It makes no difference what the papers say if you are right."

—Diary entry, January 1, 1947

Harry Truman often faced a hostile press, and it became a circumstance so routine that he could even joke about it. "Mr. President," a reporter began at a press conference on June 16, 1949, "the first thing Jefferson did was to release eleven newspaper publishers from prison." The president looked the reporter in the eye, smiled, and replied, "Yes. I think he made a mistake on that." Nevertheless, he read the papers religiously—and philosophically: "Read the morning papers as usual," he noted in his diary. "Some gave me hell and some did not. It makes no difference what the papers say if you are right."

It is impossible to lead in a vacuum, but every effective leader ultimately relies on his or her own internal moral compass. You cannot afford to ignore comment, advice, and criticism, but you cannot become enslaved to them. Consensus does not confer infallibility, and you should never permit it to coerce you to deviate from a course in which you believe.

LESSON 65
SAY WHAT NEEDS SAYING

"But it needs to be said."

—Diary entry, February 2, 1948

Harry Truman himself occasionally remarked that he was not the likeliest of champions for racial equality, having been raised in a Confederate-leaning part of Missouri by a mother he described as "unreconstructed." But the fact is that Truman was the first American president after Abraham Lincoln to take a decisive stand on civil rights and racial justice.

As early as 1939, when he was a senator, Truman successfully sponsored a bill to allow black pilots to serve in the Civilian Pilot Training Program of the U.S. Army Air Corps. This became the basis of the wartime Army Air Force program that trained the celebrated "Tuskegee airmen," the cadre of African-American fighter pilots who served in a segregated unit with the Fifteenth Air Force in North Africa and the Mediterranean and who could take pride in never having lost a bomber from formations they escorted to and from enemy targets.

In 1946, Truman created the President's Committee on Civil Rights, which the following year produced the landmark report *To Secure These Rights*. Based on that report, Truman delivered to Congress a special "Civil Rights Message," calling for a joint congressional committee on civil rights and for the creation of a civil rights division in the Department of Justice. He also asked for a Fair Employment Practices Commission to end racial discrimination in employment, and for federal protection of voting rights and a federal antilynching law.

Truman knew that the conservative Congress would like none of this. "I sent Congress a Civil Rights message," he wrote in his diary on February 2, 1948. "They no doubt will receive it as coldly as they did my State of the Union message. But it needs to be said."

Conservative Republicans were generally opposed to federal civil rights legislation, but so were many Southern Democrats. Indeed, it was Truman's advocacy of such a program that helped drive the formation of the breakaway wing of Southern Democrats in 1948, the segregationist "Dixiecrats," led by Senator Strom Thurmond of South Carolina. To Truman, none of this mattered. He knew only too well that Congress would give him little of what he asked for. That didn't matter, either. What he said needed to be said.

Beyond *saying* what needed to be said, as chief executive Truman *did* what he could do. Only Congress can make laws, but the president can issue executive orders, and on July 26, 1948, President Truman issued Executive Order 9981, directing that "all persons in the Armed Services" were to receive "equality of treatment and opportunity . . . without regard to race." Truman did not use the word *integration* in the order, but when a reporter asked him if that is what the order meant, the president replied with his usual directness: "Yes."

LESSON 66

CALL THEIR BLUFF

*"On the 26th day of July, which out in Missouri we call
'Turnip Day,' I am going to call Congress back and ask them to
pass laws to halt rising prices, to meet the housing crisis—which
they are saying they are for in their platform."*

—"Address in Philadelphia Upon Accepting the Nomination of the Democratic National Convention," July 15,
1948

During the hard-fought election campaign of 1948, Truman responded to a host of promises made in the Republican Party platform by calling an adjourned Congress back into session on July
26—Missouri's "Turnip Day"—and challenging them to enact
the legislation they promised:

> At the same time I shall ask them to act upon other vi-
> tally needed measures such as aid to education, which
> they say they are for; a national health program; civil
> rights legislation, which they say they are for; an in-
> crease in the minimum wage, which I doubt very much
> they are for; extension of the social security coverage
> and increased benefits, which they say they are for;
> funds for projects needed in our program to provide
> public power and cheap electricity. . . .
> I shall ask for adequate and decent laws for dis-

placed persons in place of this anti-Semitic, anti-Catholic law which this 80th Congress passed.

Now, my friends, if there is any reality behind that Republican platform, we ought to get some action from a short session of the 80th Congress. They can do this job in 15 days, if they want to do it. They will still have time to go out and run for office.

They are going to try to dodge their responsibility. They are going to drag all the red herrings they can across this campaign, but I am here to say that [Truman's running mate] Senator [Alben] Barkley and I are not going to let them get away with it.

Now, what that worst 80th Congress does in this special session will be the test. The American people will not decide by listening to mere words, or by reading a mere platform. They will decide on the record, the record as it has been written. . . .

There is a test for all claims, pledges, and promises—it is *performance*—and it speaks louder and clearer than the most eloquent of speeches. It is not sufficient merely to set policy and define goals for the organization. As a leader, you must also follow through by monitoring, coaxing, motivating, and shaping performance—the progress of the enterprise in the *execution* of policy and the *pursuit* of goals.

LESSON 67
GIVE 'EM HELL

"Give 'em hell, Harry!"

—Campaign cry of 1948

If any presidential candidate ever had the right to be defeatist, surely Truman was the man in 1948. Just about everyone was certain he'd lose to the Republican governor of New York, Thomas E. Dewey. Pollster Elmo Roper was so sure that, on September 9, 1948, he announced that he would conduct no more Roper Polls concerning the election. "My whole inclination," he commented, "is to predict the election of Thomas E. Dewey by a heavy margin and devote my time and efforts to other things."

Truman appreciated just how bad things looked, but he refused to give up. Taking note of the smug Republican overconfidence that prompted Dewey to run an ultra-low-profile campaign, Truman resolved to conduct an all-out person-to-person appeal. To running mate Alben Barkley he pledged that he would go out and "give 'em hell." This phrase was never crafted intentionally as a campaign slogan, but it soon leaked out and became a battle cry among Truman's supporters during his spectacular whistle-stop tour in his special Pullman car, the *Ferdinand Magellan*. At virtually every one of 356 stops, the candidate was greeted with "Give 'em hell, Harry!" and went on to stun both the pollsters and the Republicans by winning, 24,105,812 popular votes to Dewey's 21,970,065, even with the breakaway "Dixiecrat" candidacy of segregationist Strom Thurmond, who captured 1,169,021 votes.

Any campaign can *end* in failure, but it is in your hands not to let the campaign *begin* that way. The greatest defeat is the absence of an attempt. Why seal your fate with surrender at the outset? Try—hard.

LESSON 68
CHALLENGE CRITICS

"If those groups attacking our foreign policy and Mr. Acheson have any alternative policies to offer, they should disclose them. They owe it to their country."

—Radio speech, December 15, 1950

After the sudden and massive incursion of Chinese Communist troops into North Korea, the Korean War reached a level of extreme crisis. U.S.-led United Nations forces were in full retreat deep into the south. President Truman broadcast a speech to the nation (as he wrote in his memoirs) "to tell my fellow countrymen what we faced and what we would have to do." In the speech, by way of responding to "groups attacking our foreign policy and [Secretary of State Dean] Acheson," Truman challenged the critics to propose "alternative policies."

One of the most effective ways to deal with critics is to challenge—or invite—their positive and creative contribution. This is a call to put up or shut up. Criticism without creativity and the offer of a plausible alternative is not criticism at all, but mere carping and sniping. At best, such criticism is idle; at worst, it is destructive.

A challenge to a critic might actually elicit a viable alternative idea or some other positive contribution to the ongoing dialogue. This is not a cause for embarrassment, but a highly desirable outcome. Your objective in challenging a critic is not to crush him or personally to win the day, but to create a victory for your organization. If the challenge silences the critic, so be it. But if it proves of value and creates a benefit for the enterprise, thank the creative complainer and be happy he's part of the group.

LESSON 69
AUTHORITY: DON'T GIVE IT UP TO A DUMB SON OF A BITCH

"I fired [General Douglas MacArthur] because he wouldn't respect the authority of the President. . . . I didn't fire him because he was a dumb son of a bitch, although he was, but that's not against the law for generals. If it was, half to three quarters of them would be in jail."

—Interview with Merle Miller, 1961, in *Plain Speaking: An Oral Biography of Harry S. Truman*

Whether to supervisors or CEOs, it happens all the time: A subordinate fails to be subordinate. Occasionally the lapse is innocent and inadvertent; usually, however, it is a deliberate foray over the boss's head or behind the leader's back, a dangerous break in the chain of command or a treacherous side step around it.

MacArthur did it to Truman over Korea.

When the Korean War broke out early in the summer of 1950, Truman named General of the Army Douglas MacArthur to command the U.S.-dominated United Nations forces defending South Korea against the Communist North. The Supreme Allied Commander in the Pacific during World War II, the general who pledged "I shall return" to the American and Filipino forces on the doomed Philippines and then triumphantly redeemed that pledge, an imperious, sublimely confident "American Caesar," MacArthur was an unalloyed hero to most of his countrymen.

But MacArthur failed to grasp the profound difference between World War II and the Korean conflict, whereas Truman understood the difference only too well. The struggle in World War II called for an all-out effort, a full-out fight everywhere and every day. In Korea, half a decade later, a war of maximum effort was impossible. Hovering over Korea were the Soviet Union and Communist China. The Soviets had tested their first atomic bomb on August 29, 1949. The Chinese did not yet have nuclear weapons, but their army and population resources were overwhelming to contemplate. Press too hard in Korea, or take the battle into bordering Russia and China, and World War III might dwarf World War II in destruction, just as that conflict had eclipsed World War I. So Truman decided to fight a "limited" war, one designed to resist the Communist invasion without fanning a brushfire into a global conflagration.

The president understood that it was a dangerous game. For Douglas MacArthur, it was a game whose rules he simply could not accept. "In war," he would tell Congress in his famous farewell address of April 19, 1951, "there is no substitute for victory."

For much of the early Korean War, MacArthur commanded with brilliance, pushing the enemy across the 38th parallel dividing South from North and then continuing to push, all the way through the North, to within fifty miles of the Yalu River, the border between North Korea and Manchuria. Truman, wary, flew to Wake Island for a one-on-one meeting with MacArthur. Thus provoked, would the Chinese intervene? the president asked. No: The general declared with absolute assurance that all Chinese threats were empty. Truman therefore authorized the advance to continue.

Within days, however, it became chillingly clear that Chinese troops *had* entered the war, and on the night of November 25, 1950, massive Chinese forces hit the Eighth Army hard on its center and right. Two days later, even more powerful attacks overran other U.S. units. By November 28, U.N. positions were caving in. By December 15, U.N. forces had withdrawn all the way back to the 38th parallel.

MacArthur now sought authorization to attack China itself. Truman ordered MacArthur to contain and limit the war instead, keeping his forces within Korea. If this became untenable, he was to evacuate the Korean peninsula altogether. Over MacArthur's protests, Truman ordered a defensive strategy intended to inflict maximum casualties on the attackers. The GIs called it Operation Meatgrinder, and, slowly, it succeeded in regaining the ground south of the 38th parallel that had been lost to the Communists. On March 21, 1951, the U.N. member nations fighting the war agreed that securing South Korea below the 38th parallel was an acceptable outcome of the war.

When MacArthur learned that Truman was about to announce his willingness to begin negotiations with the Chinese and North Koreans on the basis of current positions, he undercut his commander in chief by urging the United Nations to expand the conflict instead. Enraged, Truman nevertheless wanted to avoid a strategically demoralizing open dispute with his top commander. He withheld his peace offer, pending further military developments.

Then the general crossed the line, unmistakably and irretrievably.

MacArthur wrote a letter to Representative Joseph W. Martin, saying that it was absolutely necessary to open up a second front against China itself. He wrote what he would later repeat to the Congress as a whole: There could be "no substitute for victory." Martin, a Republican who was no friend to Truman, read the letter into the *Congressional Record* on April 5, 1951.

An effective leader must learn not only to tolerate dissent among those he or she leads, but also to value that dissent, to learn from it, and to use it. But an effective leader must also recognize when dissent crosses the line into insubordination, an effort to compromise the authority without which a leader can no longer lead. After consulting his Cabinet and the Joint Chiefs of

Staff, the president relieved Douglas MacArthur as commander of United Nations forces on April 11, 1951.

Firing a national hero for wanting to a win a war: What president has ever willingly made so supremely unpopular a decision? Yet Truman made it. He made it for two very good reasons. The first was to save the world from the risk of a new world war. The second was to save the presidency: not *his* presidency alone but, as he explained years later, *the* presidency, "the authority of the President." Allow a military leader, whether a hero or a dumb son of a bitch, to usurp the authority of the president, and that authority might well be lost forever. Truman was unwilling to let such a loss be a part of the legacy he left the office of president, even if protecting the office meant—as many believed it had—personal political suicide.

A leader does not relinquish leadership.

When a White House staffer suggested to the president that he announce the decision as having been made with the unanimous concurrence of his advisers—as, indeed, it had been—Truman refused to share responsibility. "Son," he said, "not tonight. Tonight I am taking this decision on my own responsibility as president of the United States and I want nobody to think I am sharing it. Tonight it is my decision and mine alone." To share the heavy burden of responsibility that comes with leadership was, as Truman saw it, to relinquish leadership itself. And that was unacceptable.

LESSON 70
KNOW WHEN TO HOLD YOUR FIRE

*"Don't attack your opponent. Whenever you do, it only gives him
free advertising and another chance to attack you. Let him attack
you if he will, but you will be all right if you stick to the issues."*

—Letter to friend and political strategist Frank
McNaughton, October 18, 1956

Despite the epithet his supporters affectionately applied to him
during his 1948 campaign for the White House, "Give 'em Hell
Harry," Truman never directed an attack against the person of
his opponent, but focused instead on the opposition's platform,
policies, and performance. This was not just a matter of political
etiquette or decorum—although it *was* that, too—but of effective campaigning. Voters, Truman believed, are ultimately more
concerned about issues than personalities—or at least they should
be. *Issues* are about results, after all, and it is the results that shape
the welfare of the people.

It is in the best interest of any organization to keep the focus
on results—on policies, issues, problems, and opportunities—
and not on personalities. Attacking an opponent misdirects the
attention of the organization. That is bad enough, but if the attack also focuses attention on the opponent, it is even worse. Why
give the opposition publicity? Resist the impulse to go for the
jugular. Attack the facts of the matter instead.

LESSON 71
PREPARE FOR THE ICY STARE

"A president cannot always be popular. He has to be able to say yes and no, and more often no."

—*Memoirs, Volume Two: Years of Trial and Hope*

Raised in a democracy, we learn that leadership and popularity go hand in hand. Given a choice, no group deliberately chooses an unpopular man or woman as its leader. Yet the fact is that leadership often requires the courage, wisdom, and fortitude to make unpopular decisions.

Successful leadership requires a liberal dose of democratic principle. Effective leaders are very much "of the people, by the people, and for the people." Paradoxically, however, they are also *apart from* the people. While creating a bond with those they lead, they remain unmistakably separate as well.

"A man with thin skin has no business being president," Truman wrote in *Mr. Citizen*. He understood that leadership lays you open to criticism and, sometimes, much worse. It can bring on a condition that may be described as the exact opposite of popularity, casting you under the collective icy stare of the entire organization. Listen and respond to those you lead, and when yes is the best answer, answer yes. But when no is called for, don't hesitate, and endure those icy stares as long as necessary.

LESSON 72
DON'T WRESTLE A RED HERRING

"Watch out for these people who make mountains out of something that doesn't exist—not even a molehill!"

—Seminar on Statecraft, Columbia University, April 28, 1959

Effective leaders are sensitive and responsive to the concerns of those they lead. To be otherwise is to lose touch with the organization. However, as Truman counseled his Columbia University student audience in 1959, "You'll have the experience [of] people who make mountains out of something that doesn't exist—not even a molehill," and these individuals can drain your energy as well as the resources of the entire organization. Truman was always careful to distinguish issues raised by "stuffed shirts," those who made mountains out of less than molehills, from those of concern to people who were sincere and fully committed to their beliefs. He told the Columbia audience, "I don't care what your politics are, I don't care what you believe politically, and I don't care what your religion is, as long as you live by it and act by it." Only those who live and act by what they believe are worth the time and energy of the leader and the organization as a whole. As for the rest, they present nothing but red herrings, fruitless to follow and even more exhausting to wrestle with.

LESSON 73

ONE LEADER TO ANOTHER

"You know my program was 'Give 'em Hell' and if they don't like it give 'em more hell."

—Letter to John F. Kennedy, June 28, 1962

During Truman's 1948 contest as underdog against Republican candidate Thomas E. Dewey, "Give 'em hell" became the catchiest campaign slogan since 1840's "Tippecanoe and Tyler, too" (see "Give 'Em Hell," in this chapter). The slogan far outlasted the campaign, becoming an affectionate epithet attached to the man himself. For Truman, givin' 'em hell meant refusing to let up on injustice, inefficiency, corruption, and just plain wrongheadedness; refusing to tolerate complacency; and refusing to give up, period. To President Kennedy, whom he admired despite concern about his youth and inexperience, Truman wrote a letter on June 28, 1962, with simple advice: "Don't let them tell *you* what to do—you tell them, as you have!" This was in support of JFK's proposals for public welfare programs (the first stirrings of the "War on Poverty," which would be instituted under Kennedy's successor, Lyndon B. Johnson) and was intended to stiffen the young president's resolve to resist the objections of Southern Democrats ("Republicrats," Truman called them) to such programs.

Truman closed the letter with "You know my program was 'Give 'em Hell' and if they don't like it give 'em more hell." It was important advice from one leader to another, yet, as expressed in the letter, it was not quite accurate. "I never did give anybody hell," Truman was quoted during a memorial service in Congress after his death in 1972. "I just told the truth and they thought it was hell."

For leaders who would emulate "Give 'em Hell Harry," it is important to understand that givin' 'em hell is not about unconditionally forcing your own point of view on others. It is about telling the truth, no matter how hard it is on you or anybody else. It is about calling 'em as you see 'em. It is about determining the truth and deciding what is right, then sticking to it regardless of what others tell you.

There is yet one more component to givin' 'em hell in the manner of Harry Truman. "Every political battle I fight with everything I've got," Truman was quoted by Kenneth W. Thompson in *Portraits of the American Presidents: The Truman Presidency*, "and when it's over I get hold of my opponent and we have a bourbon and branch and say, 'What can we do for the country?'" The object of givin' 'em hell is not to "defeat" an "enemy," but to enable the right thing to be done. It is for the good of the nation or whatever organization you lead, and your opponents, as members of the enterprise, must share in that good.

LESSON 74
LET THEM KICK YOU AROUND

"Do you know why I go back home every once in a while? So people can kick me around."

—To David Lilienthal, director of the Tennessee Valley
Authority, quoted in Margaret Truman, *Harry S. Truman*

Too many managers and leaders insulate themselves from subordinates and others of their constituents. They strive to make themselves bulletproof, unassailable, impervious to criticism. This is understandable—after all, nobody likes to be criticized. But it is a serious error in leadership for two reasons.

First: Feedback, both positive and negative, is important for anyone charged with directing an organization. You couldn't steer your car without visual and even tactile feedback, so how can you expect to steer your enterprise in the absence of praise, complaints, and progress reports?

Second: Truman understood that most people feel remote from their government leaders. They are bureaucrats, not human beings. To remedy this, he did his best to present himself as a person, and that meant, in part, getting back home and exposing himself to frank criticism and hard questions. Truman's audiences were never handpicked or screened. Whether or not this made the president feel good or bad is not the point. What matters is that it gave the right feelings to the people he led. It empowered them by giving them access to the man in charge. Effective leaders get kicked around—not by accident, but by design.

LESSON 75
FIGHT, NATURALLY

"It's natural for a president to have problems with the Congress or the Supreme Court; in fact, it's my opinion that if a president isn't in an occasional fight with the Congress or the courts, he's not doing a good job."

—Quoted in *Where the Buck Stops: The Personal and Private Writings of Harry S. Truman* (Margaret Truman, ed.)

Some leaders and managers enjoy conflict and seem to thrive on it; most of us, however, much prefer smooth sailing. Indeed, most of us assume that a "healthy" or "normal" organization is characterized by a peaceful harmony, and we believe that conflict is abnormal, a symptom of a sick enterprise.

This is a mistake.

In any organization of even moderate complexity, it is complete harmony that is a sign of ill health. Conflict, in contrast, is healthy.

There is no point in gratuitously creating conflict, picking fights for the sake of fighting, but neither should you run away from conflict. Sometimes, it is even a good idea to stir the pot. On some issues, it is only through conflict that all the dimensions, questions, benefits, and potential pitfalls emerge. One great advantage of an organization is diversity of perception, point of view, approach, and opinion. Such diversity is not necessarily harmonious, and it is a mistake to throw away the advantages of creative disharmony in a misguided effort to transform the enterprise into a monolith.

Encourage dissent. Be willing to fight, and be willing to be fought against. That is part of a leader's job—but only part. Make sure the conflict does not simply leave people hurt and bruised but, rather, creates fresh perceptions, new ideas, and alternative approaches that benefit everyone. Don't fight to defeat your "enemies," but to preserve and promote the true health of the organization.

LESSON 76
GET A DOG

"If you want a friend in Washington, get a dog."

—Quoted in *The New York Times,* March 10, 1989

To lead is not necessarily to be loved—or hated. It is a serious mistake to look to the situation of leadership for emotional gratification of any kind. While the effective leader must be a "people person," one who understands and respects the emotional needs of others, the final focus of leadership must be on issues rather than personalities. To be sure, action on those issues will affect attitudes and emotions within the organization, but it is the issues themselves that are most important, because they are most susceptible to effective action. It is far easier to change a circumstance than it is to change a person. Fix problems, not people.

It is a mistake to regard the enterprise you lead as a "family" or a group of "friends." You already have a family, and you must look elsewhere for friends.

CHAPTER 7

BRING PEOPLE TOGETHER

LESSON 77
AN EARLY LESSON IN LEADERSHIP

"I used to watch my father and mother closely to learn what I could do to please them, just as I did with my schoolteachers and playmates. Because of my efforts to get along with my associates I usually was able to get what I wanted."

—*Memoirs, Volume One: Year of Decisions*

If you've ever envied someone's "instinctive" leadership ability, consider this early experience of Harry Truman. Here is the beginning of that instinct, which, of course, is not an instinct at all, but behavior learned through observation and experience. Like most social transactions, leadership is based on an exchange of value for value. Listen, observe, and learn what those around you need, want, and worry about, then endeavor to address these issues. In exchange, you will usually be able to get what you want.

LESSON 78
SEEK SUPPORT AND PREPARE TO DO
WITHOUT IT

*"I would rather do it with your full and understanding support
and welcome."*

—*Memoirs, Volume One: Year of Decisions*

After the death of Franklin Roosevelt in April 1945, President
Truman wanted to convene a special joint session of Congress as
soon as possible so that he could address the legislators (and the
nation) in person. He met with a group of senators and represen-
tatives, some of whom were opposed to the joint session "and
others were doubtful," although most "were in agreement." Truman noted that he "asked each one for his opinion and listened
carefully to what they had to say. I then outlined my reasons for
considering it imperative to let the nation know through Congress that I proposed to continue the policies of the late President. I felt that it was important, too, to ask for continued
bi-partisan support of the conduct of the war."

The president's explanation was persuasive, and he obtained
unanimous agreement on calling the joint session; however, one
senator remarked, "Harry, you were planning to come whether
we liked it or not."

The president replied, "You know I would have, but I would
rather do it with your full and understanding support and welcome."

This response embodied more than one aspect of Truman's
understanding of leadership. First, it made clear his grasp of the

president's power. The approval he sought was not absolutely required. Second, it communicated the strength of his will and resolve. Third, it communicated respect and regard for colleagues who lacked his special authority. Fourth, it represented a desire for a cordial and productive working relationship based on genuine collaboration. This was not a *plea* for such a relationship, but an expression of *preference*. As such, it affirmed rather than compromised the president's authority.

Without compromising any of your authority, look for ways to create a collegial and collaborative climate, which is almost always the most productive environment in which to work.

LESSON 79
CONSIDER YOUR "CUSTOMERS"

"Another hectic day in the executive office. Saw a lot of customers. Hope they all left happy. Most of 'em did. . . ."

—Diary entry, June 5, 1945

In the diary Truman kept during his years in the White House, he habitually referred to those who came to see him in the Oval Office as "customers." Doubtless there was more than a touch of humor in the choice of words of a former haberdasher, but there was also plenty of earnest behind the joke. Truman did not think of those who sought his time or his help as "dignitaries" or "statesmen" or "officials" or "petitioners" or "politicians" or "office seekers," but as *customers*.

Just what does it mean to think of those you lead or work with as your "customers"?

In the simplest and most literal sense, of course, a customer is someone who obtains from you a product or service in exchange for money. Looked at a bit more abstractly, a customer is someone who expects value for value. In April 1959, the former president gave a series of lectures and seminars at Columbia University. Greeted warmly by his audience of students and professors, he remarked: "I'm highly complimented and highly pleased, and I hope you'll be as happy when I get through with you as you were when I came in [*laughter*]. It's always nice to have a grand reception, but it's much nicer to have a bunch of satisfied customers once you get through."

154

Your object is to create "customer satisfaction," not just for its own sake, but so that your customers will return and exchange further value for value. This arrangement is as important in a government or a business as it is in a haberdashery—or a university lecture.

As a leader, your responsibility is to create satisfaction among those you lead, to give them value in return for the value you require of them. This is a distinctly economic system, a cycle of give and take. Allow it to become a one-way process—in which you or others do nothing but give or nothing but take—and the cycle will break down and cease to function. Truman avoided this fatal situation by persisting in thinking of subordinates, colleagues, and, ultimately, the people of the United States as his customers. Consider a similar adjustment in your vocabulary and the thinking behind it.

LESSON 80
NEVER PRACTICE PUNITIVE
MANAGEMENT

"When the underdog gets power, he too often turns out to be an even more brutal top dog."

—Memoirs, Volume One: Year of Decisions

With victory won in Europe, Truman was anxious not to repeat the errors of the Treaty of Versailles, which had ended World War I by imposing on Germany economic ruin and political humiliation. These punitive measures created a climate of rage and hopelessness that spawned the likes of Adolf Hitler and virtually ensured that World War I would be followed by World War II. Truman wrote, "I did not approve of reducing Germany to an agrarian state," as some American and European diplomats proposed. This "could starve Germany to death," which would be "an act of revenge, and too many peace treaties had been based on that spirit." Truman did not want to make Germany an underdog, which would likely repeat the two-decade process that had played out between World Wars I and II, and, when it did manage to regain power, put Germany in position to become "an even more brutal top dog."

Management based on punitive principles may (or may not) achieve desired short-term results, but, in the long run, it creates fears and resentments that poison an organization. Do not allow the enterprise to become a network of personal power relationships. Manage results, not personalities. Reward positive results, and endeavor to correct negative ones. Threaten or punish no one. In the worst case, remove from the organization those who consistently produce unacceptable results.

LESSON 81
CHANGE *SHOULD* TO *MUST*

"The key sentence . . . read, 'I believe that it should be the policy of the United States. . . . ' I took my pencil, scratched out 'should' and wrote in 'must.'"

—Memoirs, Volume Two: Years of Trial and Hope

In the aftermath of World War II, during March 1946, the people of Greece held their first election since 1936. In protest, however, the far left wing abstained, and the royalist right-wing slate was carried to victory. The new government issued a plebiscite by which King George II was returned to the Greek throne. Six months later, the king died and was succeeded by his brother Paul. In this unsettled political climate, the left wing made a bid for power, and the country was plunged into civil war. In October 1946, Greek Communists created the Democratic Army, which backed the establishment of a Communist Provisional Democratic Government. The Greek Communists were a small minority, but they drew support from the international Communist bloc and were thereby able to obtain control of much of northern Greece.

Spurred by the situation in Greece, President Truman resolved to pursue a policy of "containing" communism, the objective of which was to oppose and block the expansion of communism wherever in the world such expansion threatened. Pursuant to this policy, on March 12, 1947, the president addressed a joint session of Congress and delivered the most important speech of his career and one of the most important speeches of the twentieth century. He proclaimed as the policy of the United States support for "free peoples" in their fight against subversion, especially Communist-sponsored subversion. The press dubbed this the "Truman Doctrine," a term Truman himself never liked, but which stuck anyway.

In working with his advisers and writers to prepare the speech, Truman was keenly aware of its great consequence. He rejected a first draft: "The writers had filled the speech with all sorts of background data and statistical figures about Greece and made the whole thing sound like an investment prospectus." Truman returned the draft to Secretary of State Dean Acheson, asking him for more emphasis on general policy. The president was anxious that Congress and the American people understand that he was proposing not merely helping Greece, but taking an enduring ideological stand for the very highest stakes. When the new draft was returned to him, Truman found it "half-hearted. The key sentence, for instance, read, 'I believe that it should be the policy of the United States. . . . ' I took my pencil, scratched out 'should' and wrote in 'must.'" He made similar edits throughout the document: "I wanted no hedging in this speech. This was America's answer to the surge of expansion of Communist tyranny. It had to be clear and free of hesitation or double talk."

Any leadership decision should be carefully weighed and considered, with all shadings and subtleties taken into account. But once the decision is made, its announcement must be clear, unambiguous, and wholehearted in its vigor. The contemplation and formulation of policy is a process of much back-and-forth movement, expressing doubts and second thoughts. The execution of policy, however, must move in one direction only. Contemplation includes a host of *shoulds*. Execution can admit only *musts*.

LESSON 82
MAKE COMMON CAUSE WITH COMMON SENSE

"I'm going to make a common sense, intellectually honest campaign. It will be a novelty—and it will win."

—Diary entry, July 16, 1948

Almost to a man, pollsters and pundits wrote off Truman's chances for victory against New York governor Thomas E. Dewey in the 1948 run for the White House. Truman, in contrast, always believed he would win. He classed Dewey, along with Teddy Roosevelt and even Franklin Delano Roosevelt (a president he generally considered among the very greatest), as a "fakir." Dewey, Truman wrote in his diary, "synthetically milks cows and pitches hay for the cameras just as that other fakir, Teddy Roosevelt, did. . . . I don't believe the USA wants any more fakirs—Teddy and Franklin are enough."

Truman's alternative?

"So I'm going to make a common sense, intellectually honest campaign. It will be a novelty—and it will win."

A *fakir* is a Moslem or Hindu religious ascetic and mendicant, who typically makes his living by performing feats of magic or demonstrating apparently supernatural endurance. Most English speakers tend to associate the word with *faker*—although there is no actual linguistic connection—and that is something of the sense Truman intended with regard to Dewey and the two Roosevelts. They were not above dazzling the public with elaborate displays and gestures that were not altogether and at all times genuine. In his time, each was regarded as a master politician, and in 1948 the smart money was squarely on Dewey. But Truman's instinct was to redefine political appeal, not as the magic of a fakir, but as the hard, honest work of common sense. Instead of trying to dazzle the public, he resolved to take his message—a straightforward presentation of facts, a contrast between the Democratic and Republican platforms—directly to the public. This was the motive behind his spectacular cross-country whistle-stop campaign. Of course, against all expectations—except his own—Truman won. In the end, the most effective way to make common cause is to make common sense.

LESSON 83
MAINTAIN A POSITIVE PERSPECTIVE

"Most all the people in the USA are kindly happy people. . . ."

—Diary entry, November 5, 1950

Truman did not allow the assassination attempt of November 1, 1950 (for the story, see "Live What You Believe," in Chapter 5), to skew his reading of the American people. Gratified by the reception he received in St. Louis just four days after the assassins' assault on Blair House, Truman observed that "most all the people in the USA are kindly happy people and they show it by smiling, waving and shouting. . . ." He was greeted by "the usual 'There he is!' 'Hello, Harry.'"

Just as Truman maintained his positive perspective on the American people, he also refused to lose perspective on the power of his office. He did not take the adulation personally: "People all along the way wanted to see the President—not me!" Like all good leaders, Truman never lost sight of the necessary separation between his person and his office. Cults are inherently dangerous, and most dangerous of all is a cult of personality.

LESSON 84
ENDURE THE WEATHER,
CREATE THE CLIMATE

"I wish I had straight out opposition and loyal support. I guess it is too much to ask for!"

—Diary entry, November 30, 1950

The mythical/macho motto of the Old West, "Yer either fur me or agin' me," has always appealed to some leaders. Most of us at least some of the time think in dualistic terms: good vs. evil, expensive vs. cheap, hot vs. cold, and so on. We're so accustomed to this dualism that we take it for granted as an accurate picture of the world. Of course, it is not. If they have any degree of significance or complexity, few qualities, emotions, or beliefs exist in neatly opposed pairs of black-and-white opposites. Instead, they present a spectrum.

Truman had many battles with what he called "the terrible 80th Congress." It was controlled by a Republican majority, and the president resigned himself to constant opposition. The 81st Congress, however, ushered in a Democratic majority, and, to his chagrin, Truman found "liars, trimmers and pussyfooters on both sides of the aisle in the Senate and the House." To his diary he confided, "I'm sorry. I wish I had straight out opposition and loyal support. I guess it is too much to ask for!"

Resist the temptation to define your leadership between stark poles of support and opposition. Your situation is usually more complicated than that and is shaded by time and changing circumstances, as well as by collective and individual moods, anxieties, and enthusiasms. The weather of your organization may change from day to day. You can cope with it, but you can't fight it. Your job is not to change the weather, but to create an enduring climate subject not to this or that breeze, a passing high, or a lingering low, but moored by clearly defined principles and worthwhile objectives.

LESSON 85
PROVE PROGRESS

"But so far it has been successful."

—"Radio Report to the American People on Korea and on
U.S. Policy in the Far East," April 11, 1951

Following by a very few years the Allied triumph in World War
II, the Korean War was bitterly bewildering to many Americans.
The war that ended in 1945 had been an all-out campaign
against evil, with total victory the only acceptable outcome,
whereas the conflict in Korea, fought in an obscure corner of the
world, was conducted as a frustratingly limited effort, lest a new
world war result.

Faced with a complex, frustrating process, a leader must define or redefine objectives and goals and report on progress toward them. This is essential to maintaining the group's will and
commitment to continue. Truman handled the task masterfully:

> The question we have had to face is whether the Com-
> munist plan of conquest can be stopped without a
> general war. Our Government and other countries as-
> sociated with us in the United Nations believe that the
> best chance of stopping it without a general war is to
> meet the attack in Korea and defeat it there.
>
> That is what we have been doing. It is a difficult
> and bitter task.
>
> But so far it has been successful.

So far, we have prevented World War III.

So far, by fighting a limited war in Korea, we have prevented aggression from succeeding, and bringing on a general war. And the ability of the whole free world to resist Communist aggression has been greatly improved.

In these few sentences, Truman laid out the chief objective—to stop Communist aggression without provoking world war—and then stated that we have been doing just this. He expressed what were doubtless the sentiments of his listeners—"It is a difficult and bitter task"—but asserted that "so far" the task has been performed successfully. The implication was unmistakable. The job is not finished, but just because it is not finished does not mean it has failed. "So far," it has succeeded, and Truman provided evidence: World War III has been prevented, and the ability of the free world to resist Communist aggression has been "greatly improved."

You cannot always achieve triumphant closure. Indeed, most human affairs, including business, are open-ended and subject to detour and diversion. This is no cause for despair. Rather, identify progress in the journeys you lead, and clearly and honestly report that progress—however incomplete—to the members of your enterprise.

LESSON 86
SHARE A SECRET

"I would like to read to you from a secret intelligence report...."

— "Radio Report to the American People on Korea and on U.S. Policy in the Far East," April 11, 1951

The strongest platform from which to lead is trust. A leader always asks the members of the organization to trust him; however, it is far more effective to do more than merely *ask* for trust. Secure the trust of the group by demonstrating your trust in them. Open closed doors. Share a secret.

In his radio speech on Korea, President Truman told his audience that the "attack on Korea was part of a greater plan for conquering all of Asia." He did not expect his listeners to accept this without evidence, and so he continued:

> I would like to read to you from a secret intelligence report which came to us after the attack on Korea. It is a report of a speech a Communist army officer in North Korea gave to a group of spies and saboteurs last May, one month before South Korea was invaded. The report shows in great detail how this invasion was part of a carefully prepared plot. Here, in part, is what the Communist officer, who had been trained in Moscow, told his men: "Our forces," he said, "are scheduled to attack South Korean forces about the

middle of June. .... The coming attack on South Korea marks the first step toward the liberation of Asia."

Notice that he used the word "liberation." This is Communist double-talk meaning "conquest."

Deciding just what information can be shared with the group may require a carefully considered judgment. While it is true that most organizations possess information that should not be freely aired, it is also a fact that, given a choice, most managers and leaders automatically choose to keep most information unreasonably and unnecessarily close. The choice should not be automatic. Think through the situation: What doors can be opened? What secrets shared? Often, these "secrets" are more valuable revealed than kept, for the revelation purchases that most valuable of commodities, trust.

LESSON 87
PERSUASION IS EXPLANATION

"I went to the people. . . ."

—Personal memorandum, January 10, 1952

Thomas J. Pendergast was born in 1872 in St. Joseph, Missouri, and entered politics at the ground level in Kansas City in 1893, working for local precinct captains. By 1916, Pendergast was the undisputed political boss of Kansas City Democrats. He created a political machine that controlled not only municipal politics, but state politics as well, and that became a powerful influence on the national Democratic Party. During the quarter-century reign of "Boss" Pendergast, Kansas City thrived economically, but also acquired a reputation for political corruption and widespread vice and crime.

No political figure in Missouri got very far without the approval and support of the Pendergast machine, and Harry S. Truman was no exception. It was Pendergast who helped him launch his political career in 1922, when Truman ran successfully for county judge, and it was Pendergast who backed, albeit reluctantly, Truman's successful run for the Senate in 1934.

Despite his association with Pendergast, Truman earned, first on the county level and then in the U.S. Senate, a reputation for scrupulous honesty and genuine dedication to public service. Pendergast's initial reluctance to support Truman as a senatorial candidate was a testament to Truman's incorruptibility. He could not be bought, and he could not be pushed around. Yet Truman remained personally loyal to Tom Pendergast, whom he considered a mentor and friend. When Pendergast was convicted of income-tax evasion on income of $443,550, which allegedly included $315,000 in bribes, he was sentenced to federal prison in May 1939. Despite this public disgrace, Truman never denounced Pendergast, and he was one of very few in attendance at his friend's funeral in January 1945.

At the end of 1951, scandal erupted in the Bureau of Internal Revenue (predecessor of the Internal Revenue Service), which prompted Truman to fire an assistant attorney general, T. Lamar Caudle, and the general counsel of the bureau, Charles Oliphant. In response to calls for an outside investigator, Truman appointed Newbold Morris, who operated so ham-handedly that, without consulting Truman, Attorney General J. Howard McGrath fired him. Never one to allow his authority to be abridged, Truman, in turn, fired McGrath. In the resulting atmosphere of recrimination, Truman's critics resurrected his longtime association with Pendergast. As was his habit when complex crises or issues arose, Truman sat down to compose a memorandum to himself, in this case setting out the facts of his association with the late Kansas City boss.

Truman mentioned in particular an incident from 1928. In that year, the Pendergast machine, in the name of Kansas City, "decided to ask for an election to authorize a bond issue for traffic ways, an auditorium, a city hall, a sewer system and several other things including a water plant and the purchase of a bridge across the Missouri River." As county judge—in Missouri an office equivalent to county commissioner—Truman "decided to ask for a County bond issue, at the same time for a road system, two new Court Houses, and a County hospital. Pendergast told me that a County bond issue would not carry." In 1928 Missouri, this was tantamount to an order forbidding Truman to ask for the bond issue. Instead of meekly obeying, however, Truman responded by telling Pendergast "that if I told the voters how I would handle it . . . it would carry."

With that, he "went to the people":

[I] told them that I would appoint a bi-partisan board of engineers to oversee the road construction and that I would employ the two best known firms of architects in town to handle the building program, with a consulting architect from out of the State.

The county bond issue carried by a three fourths majority instead of the required two thirds. I appointed the engineers and the local architects. Then I took my private car—not a county one—and drove to Shreveport, Denver, Houston, Racine, Milwaukee, Buffalo, Brooklyn, Lincoln, Baton Rouge and several other places and looked at the new public buildings, met the architects and contractors, inspected the buildings and finally decided to employ the architect of the Court House at Shreveport as consulting architect for our county buildings.

Even now, Pendergast attempted to intervene:

When the Court was ready to let the first road contracts Mr. Pendergast called me and told me that he was in trouble with the local road contractors and would I meet with them and talk with them. I told him I would. I met them with T.J.P. present. They gave me the old song and dance about being local citizens and taxpayers and that they should have an inside track to the construction contracts.

I told them that the contracts would be let to the lowest bidders wherever they came from and that the specifications would be adhered to strictly.

The combination of moving public opinion by talking to the public and building on a hard-earned and scrupulously maintained reputation for integrity proved more persuasive in the short term and more enduring in the long run than the arm-twisting, palm-greasing tactics of machine politics. As Truman noted, "After 8 years as Presiding Judge I left the County with a road system equal to any in the country, refinanced its floating debt and [gained approval for] a set of public buildings that the people could be proud of."

The art of persuasion, a vital skill for any leader, does not require the silver tongue of a great orator. The most effective form of persuasion is explanation.

LESSON 88
BE INTERESTED IN *THEM*

"I went down there this time since I was out of office and not running for office to show them I was just interested in them."

—Letter to former Secretary of State Dean Acheson,
October 2, 1953

Newly former President Truman traveled to the little Missouri hamlet of Caruthersville to make a speech on education. Why go there? He explained the reason to Dean Acheson: "I have been going down to Caruthersville for twenty or twenty-five years because that southeast corner of Missouri has always been in my corner politically and I went down there this time since I was out of office and not running for office to show them I was just interested in them."

Just about anyone, with study and practice, can learn how to manipulate people, but it takes humanity and character to be "just interested in them." This kind of bond cannot be faked, and it is indispensable to effective leadership.

LESSON 89
MAKE YOURSELF REAL

"The people want to see the man they are voting for and they want to know what he stands for. My approach to the thing was always to explain the principles on which I was running."

—Letter to Frank McNaughton, October 18, 1956

Harry Truman was justly celebrated as a great campaigner, and in his later years any number of politicians and political strategists sought his advice. That advice was invariably simple. To Frank McNaughton, campaign manager for an Illinois senatorial candidate, he explained that voters want to see their candidate and "they want to know what he stands for"; therefore, get out, make personal appearances, and *explain your principles.*

As a leader, you are up for election every day. On paper, your authority may come from a job description, a contract, a board of directors, or a controlling financial interest, but in fact your authority is subject to a continual referendum. You remain effective as a leader only as long as the members of the organization are willing to be led by you. It is crucial, therefore, that you make yourself real to all of your constituents—subordinates, outside customers, investors—and do so on a continual basis. Constituents must see you and understand your principles. This requires visibility within the organization and a willingness to communicate. The old-school approach—"theirs is not to reason why"—is dangerous to the organization as well as to its leader. Be there, and explain yourself.

LESSON 90
BEGIN WITH THOSE WHO HAVE
THE CLOUT TO HELP YOU

"Well, there are always leaders in the Congress, the same as there are in any other organization, and almost always those leaders are reasonable men. When the President has a real program and he wants to put it over very badly, why then he sends for those leaders and discusses the matter."

—Speech at Columbia University, April 27, 1959

A student attending Truman's 1959 speech and seminar program at Columbia University wanted to know from the former president "how you can work with a Congress that is not of your party and somewhat opposed to your policies." Truman replied simply and directly. You begin by sending for the congressional leaders of both parties and discuss the issues with them.

Opposition can be an overwhelming prospect for any leader. The first task is not to attack the opposition, but to take steps to reduce opposition to manageable proportions. The most effective way of doing this in any organization is to identify the leaders on all sides of the issue at hand, then engage them in frank discussion. Make your case to these leaders. Sell it to them. Make common cause with them. Then let them bring the other members of the organization into line. The most effective means of building consensus and acting quickly is to appeal to those with the power to help you. Begin there.

LESSON 91
TAKE POSITIVE POSITIONS

"I don't believe in anti-anything. A man has to have a program; you have to be for something, otherwise you will never get anywhere."

—Seminar on Statecraft, Columbia University, April 28, 1959

In the short term, it may be relatively easy to build a consensus *against* something or someone, but such negatively based coalitions are difficult to maintain for long. Far better to identify positive issues and objectives around which to make common cause and build an effective, focused organization.

LESSON 92
ATTACK ISSUES, NOT PEOPLE

"I had unintentionally humiliated the young man."

—Quoted in Margaret Truman, *Harry S. Truman*

In the early 1960s, Truman lectured at a California college. In a question-and-answer session, a cocky young man asked the speaker what he thought of "our local yokel," meaning Governor Pat Brown. Truman responded with a curt criticism of the student's disrespect for the office of governor. Then he noticed that his words nearly brought the young man to tears. When the Q&A was over, Truman sought out the student, shook his hand, and explained that his criticism had been directed at the principle involved, not at him personally.

Truman had a reputation for the bluntest honesty, yet he always endeavored to direct his blows at issues, not individuals. In any organization, issues come and go from day to day and moment to moment, but people are long-term assets. As a leader or manager, you must from time to time criticize and correct, but to create and maintain common cause within the organization, you must ensure that your comments, sharp as they may be, are aimed at issues, not at people.

In the case of the student, Truman was so concerned (as he later told his daughter) "that I had unintentionally humiliated that young man [and that] the memory of my harsh tone might scar his whole life and ruin his reputation among his friends and acquaintances" that he asked the dean to keep him informed of the young man's progress, and he made it his business to correspond with the student.

LESSON 93
YOU CAN USUALLY DO SOMETHING

"Sure it's not a problem I can solve."

—Quoted in Ken Hechler, *Working with Truman:*
A Personal Memoir of the White House Years

Is it realistic for leaders or managers to assume they can always solve whatever problems present themselves? Of course not. But that doesn't mean a leader cannot do *something*.

When four Iowans wanted to discuss with Truman a problem with local roads and bridges, the president listened, made some suggestions, and the group left greatly satisfied. Robert Dennison, an aide present during the discussion, expressed amazement, first that President Truman would address a matter over which he had no jurisdiction and in which he could take no direct action, and, second, that the visitors had left happy, even though their problem hadn't been solved.

"Sure it's not a problem I can solve," Truman explained to Dennison. "It isn't a national problem, and maybe to you it isn't a problem, but believe me, to these people it's a problem. I'm the president of the United States and I should listen to people like that who are in trouble, even if that's all I can do."

"I do not approve of 'front porch' campaigns," Truman wrote in the second volume of his memoirs, *Years of Trial and Hope.* "I never liked to see any man elected to office who did not go out and meet the people in person and work for their votes." A leader makes common cause with those he leads by listening. Listening requires, first, a willingness to "get around" and, second, an even greater willingness to stop talking. The first requires ample energy; the second, an abundance of mature character.

Although there is no denying that a big part of leadership is problem solving, an even bigger part is listening to problems. Sometimes that's all a leader can do, and while it isn't enough, it is a great deal. Members of the enterprise look to the leader for solutions, but first they look for the leader's concern. They crave and they expect responsiveness. Confronted with a problem you know you cannot solve, your natural impulse may be to back away. Resist the impulse and embrace the problem instead. Simply by listening, you take some degree of ownership of the problem and thereby relieve part of the burden it represents. Listening to a problem does not obligate you to solve it (although you will try your best and, at the very least, encourage others to solve it if you cannot). But, as a leader, you are always obligated to listen.

LESSON 94
ADJUST YOUR PERSPECTIVE

"It's a recession when your neighbor loses his job; it's a depression when you lose your own."

—Quoted in Elizabeth Frost, *The Bully Pulpit: Quotations from American Presidents*

Truth is rarely absolute. Usually, it is a matter of perspective, as Truman's famous quip on recession versus depression illustrates. Like most of Truman's jokes, this one had a larger purpose. The lesson here is that while a leader should arbitrate what is true and what is right in order to make decisions and formulate policy, he should also concede that neither he nor anyone else has a monopoly on truth and right, and that it is often necessary to exercise sufficient imagination to see the same set of facts from multiple perspectives. An effective leader has an empathic imagination and is willing to give it free rein.

LESSON 95
BE STRONG IN RESTRAINT

"An excessive show of authority can easily degenerate into toughness for its own sake, just to show who's boss."

—Quoted in *Where the Buck Stops: The Personal and Private Writings of Harry S. Truman* (Margaret Truman, ed.)

In his discussion of George Washington in the posthumously published *Where the Buck Stops*, Truman praised the first president for his vigorous response to the so-called Whiskey Rebellion, a 1791 tax revolt in Pennsylvania: "He sent 15,000 soldiers into Pennsylvania and showed up in person to review the troops, a simple and pointed show of federal strength, and the rioting stopped and the people of Pennsylvania paid the tax like everybody else." When Washington's imperious secretary of the treasury, Alexander Hamilton, decided to underscore this demonstration of the power of central government by arresting those he deemed the ringleaders of the revolt, Washington responded by issuing pardons to all the men.

Failure to assert authority sooner or later destroys leadership; however, a punitive approach, the exercise of power for its own sake, is even more destructive. It dissolves the bonds of common cause and leads not merely to an erosion of leadership, but to the dissolution of the organization itself. The strong leader is strongest in restraint.

LESSON 96
TAKE THE TROUBLE TO TALK

"[President Washington] just talked to the people and explained things."

—Quoted in *Where the Buck Stops: The Personal and Private Writings of Harry S. Truman* (Margaret Truman, ed.)

Truman, who achieved election to the presidency in his own right by tirelessly campaigning cross-country, was impressed with the first American president's willingness to travel by stagecoach and on horseback throughout the new nation for the purpose of talking to the people and "explain[ing] things" to them, directly and in person. Like Truman's own whistle-stop campaign, this was very hard work and made an inordinate demand on Washington's time. But he did it, and he did it because he would have agreed with Truman that "every president ought to make it his business to give the people an exact outline of what his program is and why he wants it."

Wade into the organization you lead. Ask questions. Invite questions. Find out—directly—what most concerns your constituents. Communicate—directly—what most concerns you.

LESSON 97
SELLING THE IDEA

"Leadership is the art of getting other people to run with your idea as if it were their own."

—Quoted in *The Wit and Wisdom of Politics* (Chuck Henning, ed.)

Consider this cliché: *Sell the idea.* Force yourself, if you can, to take a fresh look at this stale phrase.

What does it mean to *sell*?

To sell is to bring about a change of ownership. It is to persuade someone to sacrifice something in order to acquire ownership of something else, to make that thing his or her own. To sell an idea, therefore, is to persuade others to acquire ownership of the idea, to make it their own—and to make whatever sacrifices that acquisition entails.

Truman regarded such salesmanship as the very definition of leadership. Dictators impose their ideas on others, forcibly and under duress. In contrast, leaders *sell* their ideas, exchanging value for value in return and transferring ownership in the process.

CHAPTER 8

MAKE UP YOUR MIND

LESSON 98
ALWAYS BACK THE RIGHT STUFF

"He was of the right stuff. . . . I have no apology to make."

—On supporting a Republican candidate for county marshal, quoted in Alfred Steinberg, *The Man from Missouri: The Life and Times of Harry S. Truman*

While still a local Missouri politician, Harry Truman stunned fellow Democrats by throwing his support behind John Miles, Republican candidate for county marshal. Truman justified his decision by pointing out that Miles, his commanding officer on the Western Front during World War I, had acquitted himself with great courage and resolve, holding off an attack by a superior German force. Truman answered charges that he was being disloyal to his party by explaining that Miles "was of the right stuff, and a man who wouldn't vote for his comrade under circumstances such as these would be untrue to his country. I know that every soldier understands it. I have no apology to make for it."

In any organization, loyalty is both a cement and a lubricant, essential to the structure and function of the enterprise. However, it is important to invest loyalty only in those who manifest the "right stuff," and it is even more important to act in accordance with that loyalty. It is a simple decision to make, although not always an easy one.

LESSON 99
SOMETIMES YOU DON'T
NEED PERFECTION

"It was important for us to make a start, no matter how imperfect."

—Memoirs, Volume One: Year of Decisions

Harry S. Truman took the oath of office and became president of the United States at 7:09 P.M. on April 12, 1945, about ninety minutes after he had been told of Franklin Roosevelt's death. After the oath had been administered, photographs were taken, and "those present . . . gripped my hand—often without a word, so great were their pent-up emotions." Then Truman conferred with the Cabinet and others. Presidential press secretary Steve Early informed Truman that the press wanted to know if the San Francisco conference on the creation of the United Nations, scheduled for April 25, would take place as planned.

"I did not hesitate a second," Truman recalled, and told Early that the conference would be held as President Roosevelt had directed. "I wanted to make it clear that I attached the greatest importance to the establishment of international machinery for the prevention of war and the maintenance of peace. . . . It was important for us to make a start, no matter how imperfect."

Careful planning is important to the success of any great project; sometimes, though, some issues are so pressing that you just need to get started, even with imperfect plans or incomplete resources. Reckless acts do not flow from sound leadership, of course, but the trait that is common to all effective leaders is an *imperative* to act. The essence of leadership is action, not contemplation, debate, or caution. Try never to allow the best to become the enemy of the good. Perfection is not a property of the sphere of human action, and a great part of leadership is wringing from a mass of imperfection a succession of tolerably good works and reasonably productive actions.

LESSON 100
MAKE MEETINGS COUNT

"My approach was different. . . ."

—*Memoirs, Volume One: Year of Decisions*

Harry Truman ran his Cabinet meetings differently from Franklin Roosevelt. "Little of real importance was discussed" at FDR's Cabinet meetings, Truman observed, because "Roosevelt usually had conferences with individual members of the Cabinet before and after the meetings, and it was then that detailed discussions usually took place." Truman's implication was that Cabinet meetings under FDR were more for show than they were genuinely productive working sessions. "My approach," Truman wrote, "was different. I had each member of the Cabinet lay important matters before the Cabinet as a whole, and each person present was given an opportunity to discuss the subjects that were under consideration and to give his views."

American businesses, big and small, are infatuated with meetings—so much so that often they are held with little forethought and to even less purpose. To meet has become as inevitable as a knee jerk. If meetings are virtually universal in American business, so is cynical ridicule of them. In too many organizations they have become a kind of empty ritual that many perceive as a waste of time.

Stop wasting time.

This does not mean you have to stop meeting. It means you have to stop wasting the meetings you have. Use them, as

Truman did, to get everyone working on the issues, problems, and opportunities that confront the organization. A meeting is an opportunity to focus the collective resources of the group to achieve specific objectives. See to it that no such opportunity is squandered.

LESSON 101
HONEST MEN CAN HONESTLY
DISAGREE

"A frank and open argument of this kind is the best form of free expression in which a President can get all points of view needed for him to make decisions."

—Memoirs, Volume One: Year of Decisions

Determining the policy that would govern regulation of America's atomic technology and secrets gave rise to heated debate, both nationally and within Truman's Cabinet. The president relished the debate, because he firmly believed that "honest men can honestly disagree" and that only through "frank and open argument" in a climate that promoted "free expression" could all points of view receive a thorough airing. This, Truman felt, was invaluable to the decision process; however, as always, while argument was free and open, the decision, when it came, "had to be mine to make."

Many leaders fear open debate and disagreement, believing this creates doubt and dissension within the organization and prompts members of the group to question the authority of management. Like most positions based on fear, this one is unproductive. By limiting discussion and disagreement, you greatly diminish the assets available in an organization. The virtue of a group is not singleness of mind, but multiplicity thereof, creating a variety of perspectives on a given issue, problem, or opportunity. There is no need to fear compromising authority by inviting free discussion, as long as it is absolutely clear that debate is open, but the decision, when it is finally made, belongs exclusively to you as the leader. Your decision, when it comes, ends the discussion.

"I would ask the Cabinet to share their counsel with me, even encouraging disagreement and argument to sharpen up the different points of view," Truman wrote. But once policy had been laid down, Cabinet members were expected to support it. "I could not permit . . . difference of opinions to be aired in public by a dissenting member of the Cabinet." No president could, Truman added.

LESSON 102
SINGLE STONE, SEVERAL BIRDS

"I suggested, without hesitation, that the official act of surrender should take place in Tokyo Bay, aboard a naval vessel, and that ship to be the U.S.S. Missouri.*"*

—*Memoirs, Volume One: Year of Decisions*

As soon as word reached the U.S. government that the Japanese were willing to accept the Potsdam Declaration—the Allies' terms of unconditional surrender—Truman's top military advisers, Admiral William D. Leahy and General George C. Marshall, asked him where he thought the formal surrender should take place.

"I suggested, without hesitation, that the official act of surrender should take place in Tokyo Bay, aboard a naval vessel, and that ship to be the U.S.S. *Missouri*."

Although the reply came "without hesitation," Truman's reasoning was well considered and multidimensional. "I thought it wise to hold the ceremony within view of the Japanese capital in order to impress the fact of defeat on the Japanese people," Truman reasoned, "but it also seemed desirable to remain offshore until we could be assured that there would be no last-minute outbursts of fanaticism." Moreover, the choice of the *Missouri*, as Truman saw it, "was an obvious one." It was "one of the newest and most powerful battleships of our fleet"—the very embodiment of the military might that had won the war—and, a personal plus for the president, "she had been named after my own state; my daughter Margaret had christened her, and I had spoken on that occasion."

Not every president would have devoted so much thought to the mere place of surrender. The German surrender in May had been formalized at a place convenient for General Eisenhower—but had to be repeated elsewhere to satisfy the Russians. This time, Truman took charge. An effective leader is unwilling to toss off any decision. There was nothing arbitrary about Truman's decision to hold the surrender ceremony aboard the *Missouri* in Tokyo Bay. It was a psychologically and politically impressive gesture, yet also provided for possibly violent contingencies. The ship was a powerful symbol of righteous might, yet also embodied a personal and human dimension that appealed to the president and that, doubtless, he believed would appeal to the American people. The most effective decisions result from careful thought about how to create maximum leverage by multiplying the beneficial effects of the decision. Never throw away the opportunity to make a good decision.

LESSON 103

BE WILLING TO TAKE
DESPERATE MEASURES

"These were drastic measures. They were against the principles I believed in, and I proposed them only as a desperate resort in an extreme emergency. . . ."

—Memoirs, Volume One: Year of Decisions

On May 23, 1946, the railroad unions called a nationwide strike, which President Truman attempted to avert by means of a compromise offer that was accepted by eighteen unions and the rail operators. Two individuals, however, the head of the Brotherhood of Locomotive Engineers and the head of the Brotherhood of Railway Trainmen, rejected the settlement.

"I saw that this was no contest between labor and management but one between a small group of men and their government." When the two men, Alvanley Johnston and A. F. Whitney, rejected Truman's personal appeals and announced their resolve to strike, the president confronted them: "You are not going to tie up the country. If this is the way you want it, we'll stop you."

On May 25, Truman addressed a joint session of Congress and requested emergency legislation to enjoin all strike activity and, most controversial of all, to authorize the president to draft into the armed forces all workers who went on strike against their government.

"These were drastic measures," Truman later wrote. "They were against the principles I believed in, and I proposed them only as a desperate resort in an extreme emergency where leaders defiantly called the workers out in a strike against the government." Fortunately, halfway through his message to Congress, Truman was handed a note announcing that the strike had been settled on the terms of the compromise Truman had earlier proposed.

Concerning desperate measures, be certain to answer two questions: First, what, exactly, makes the proposed measures desperate? Second, when is it necessary to take them? Without solid answers to these two questions, desperate measures are nothing more than desperation, period.

LESSON 104
LOOK THROUGH TO THE OTHER SIDE

"I answered my own question."

—*Memoirs, Volume Two: Years of Trial and Hope*

The "Truman Doctrine," the policy of supporting free nations against Communist insurgency and domination, moved the United States and its Western allies to make a strong stand in Germany, which had been divided after World War II into an Eastern Sector, controlled by the Soviets, and a Western Sector, controlled by the United States, Britain, and France. Berlin, the traditional capital of Germany, was deep inside the Soviet sector, but it, too, was divided into separate zones of occupation, the Soviets controlling the east, the western Allies the west. This never sat well with the Soviets, who, beginning in March 1948, initiated a policy of detaining troop trains bound for West Berlin. In response to this effort at intimidation, on June 7, 1948, the Western allies announced their intention to create a separate, permanent capitalist state of West Germany, to include West Berlin. The Soviets, in turn, responded two weeks later by blockading West Berlin, protesting that a *West* Germany could not include a city located in Soviet-controlled territory. A blockade is a military act, an act of war. Would the West back down? Or would the Berlin crisis trigger World War III?

To back down would make a mockery of the Truman Doctrine and open the door to unchecked Soviet aggression and worldwide Communist expansion. The president was determined to defy the blockade and supply West Berlin with food and fuel. "The main question was," Truman later wrote, "how could we remain in Berlin without risking all-out war?" With his eye on the objective of containing communism without provoking a third world war, Truman proposed a course of action that was neither a retreat nor armed aggression. He suggested an airlift of supplies to the surrounded city. To this, however, General Hoyt Vandenberg, chief of staff of the air force, objected. He believed that the airlift would drain air strength from other places, leaving the United States and its allies vulnerable. Truman heard Vandenberg out, then responded:

> I asked him if he would prefer to have us attempt to supply Berlin by ground convoy. Then, if the Russians resisted that effort and plunged the world into war, would not the Air Force have to contribute its share to the defense of the nation? I answered my own question: The airlift involved less risks than armed road convoys. Therefore, I directed the Air Force to furnish the fullest support possible to the problem of supplying Berlin.

Vandenberg was a very able officer and one of the principal architects of an independent air force; in this case, however, in contrast to Truman, he showed himself to be an insufficiently farsighted leader. Whereas Vandenberg saw in the airlift a short-term threat to security, Truman looked through to the other side and identified a far greater threat in the alternative to the airlift, ground convoys that would probably provoke all-out war. The neighborhood plumber who attempts to persuade a homeowner to invest in preventive maintenance would be familiar with Truman's long-term reasoning: *You can pay me now, or you can pay me a lot more later.* An effective leader bases decisions on a balance between immediate needs and long-term consequences.

As for the Berlin Airlift, it was one of the great early triumphs of the Cold War and a brilliant achievement of Vandenberg's air force. Air transports flew around the clock, making some 272,000 flights into West Berlin and completely circumventing the Soviet blockade. After 321 days of this, the Russians ended their futile effort to isolate West Berlin.

Do not allow the pressures of the moment to push you and your organization into short-term actions that jeopardize long-term principles and goals. You must respond to emergencies, but don't lose your balance in doing so. Look through the present crisis to the other side.

LESSON 105
EXPECT AN EXPLOSION

"Quite an explosion. Was expected but I had to act. Telegrams and letters of abuse by the dozens."

—Diary entry, April 10, 1951

In 1951, no American military figure, except perhaps for Dwight D. Eisenhower, was more popular with fellow citizens than General of the Army Douglas MacArthur. No one knew this better than Harry Truman and MacArthur himself. MacArthur's sense of popular and therefore political invulnerability emboldened him repeatedly to defy Truman's policy of limited warfare in Korea. As detailed in "Authority: Don't Give It Up to a Dumb Son of a Bitch," in Chapter 6, MacArthur publicly proclaimed that there was "no substitute for victory" and advocated vastly expanding the war, even into Manchuria. The president was persuaded that such an expansion would touch off World War III, and when MacArthur, in violation of Truman's explicit instructions, sent a letter to Republican House minority leader Joe Martin advocating expansion nevertheless and criticizing current policy, a letter Martin read into the *Congressional Record,* Truman noted in his diary on April 6, 1951: "This looks like the last straw. Rank insubordination. . . . I call in Gen. Marshall, Dean Acheson, Mr. Harriman and Gen. Bradley before Cabinet to discuss situation." Truman continued, "I've come to the conclusion that our Big General in the Far East must be recalled"; however, at the first meeting with members of his Cabinet and Army

Chief of Staff Omar Bradley, Truman didn't "express any opinion or make known my decision." Truman was too savvy a leader to begin a consultation by telling the others that his mind was already made up. To do so would have stifled discussion and dissent, and Truman wanted to hear opinions, even if they differed from his own. The overwhelming consensus, however, was for MacArthur's relief as supreme commander in Korea.

Truman approved recall orders on April 9, but because of a leak, the president had to issue the orders both earlier than he had wanted to and in a manner he had hoped to avoid. Truman had thought it most appropriate to send the orders through the secretary of the army, Frank Pace; because of the leak, he instead transmitted them directly to MacArthur.

In one respect, firing Douglas MacArthur had been an easy decision. He was insubordinate, and, even worse, his conduct undermined the Constitution, which provides for the complete subordination of the military to civil executive authority. Moreover, the course of action MacArthur advocated was dangerous for the world. In truth, Truman had no viable alternative to dismissal. Despite this, the president knew that firing a national hero during a terrible war crisis would inevitably bring "an explosion." Weighing the necessity of the action against its immediate popular consequences, Truman moved without hesitation. The authority of the office of president, the sanctity of the Constitution, and the safety of the world depended on it.

Truman's decision eloquently expressed the difference between leadership and demagoguery. A demagogue seeks to manipulate the organization by yielding to the sentiments and desires of its members. This is followship, not leadership. Leadership often requires unpopular decisions and, along with them, the will as well as the thickness of hide to withstand the explosions unpopular acts ignite.

LESSON 106
DO THE JOB

"The president—whoever he is—has to decide. He can't pass the buck to anybody. No one else can do the deciding for him. That's his job."

—Statement from 1952 or 1953, quoted in Ralph Keyes, *The Wit and Wisdom of Harry Truman*

As Truman saw it, to lead is to decide. For him, the two functions were very nearly one and the same, and the first always entailed the second. While it might be difficult to make a given decision on a given issue, the necessity of deciding was, for Truman, neither hard nor easy, but simply impossible to escape. "The important fact to remember," Truman wrote in the first volume of his memoirs, *Year of Decisions* (1955), "is that the President is the only person in the executive branch who has final authority, and if he does not exercise it, we may be in trouble. If he exercises his authority wisely, that is good for the country. If he does not exercise it wisely, that is too bad, but it is better than not exercising it at all." In the posthumous *Where the Buck Stops*, Truman observed: "Presidents have to make decisions if they're going to get anywhere, and those presidents who couldn't make decisions are the ones who caused all the trouble."

Truman believed that bad decisions could create problems, but the worse failure of leadership was to fail to make any decision, right or wrong, good or bad. The absence of decision is the absence of direction, which can lead only to disaster.

LESSON 107
DON'T FIGHT THE PROBLEM;
DECIDE IT

"[Secretary of State George C. Marshall] would listen for a long time without comment, but when the debates between members of his staff seemed destined to go on interminably and he could stand it no longer, he would say, 'Gentlemen, don't fight the problem; decide it.'"

—*Memoirs, Volume Two: Years of Trial and Hope*

If Harry Truman was frank in his criticism of the people he worked with, he was also unstinting with praise, and he admired no servant of the American people more than George C. Marshall, army chief of staff during World War II and secretary of state (from 1947 to 1949) and of defense (during 1950–1951) in Truman's Cabinet. Prime mover and architect of the Marshall Plan for postwar European aid and relief, which Winston Churchill memorably assessed as "the most unsordid political act in history," Marshall was a problem solver of the very highest order, and that was something Truman deeply appreciated. He marveled at Marshall's ability to elicit frank and useful debate from his staff and was equally impressed by the incisive skill with which he turned debate to decision.

Open discussion and free debate are indispensable problem-solving tools—up to a point. Fighting circumstances and complaining will not solve the problem. During discussion and debate, keep the group's collective intellect focused on a solution. The object is not to "eliminate" a problem. That is mere self-delusion, an object that cannot be obtained. The attainable and therefore only useful objective is to *work with* and *work through* the problem and thereby "decide it." Remind the group of this as frequently as necessary.

LESSON 108
BEWARE THE BRIEFING

"I believe that one of the problems of top military leaders is that too many of them come to rely on 'briefing.'"

—*Memoirs, Volume Two: Years of Trial and Hope*

Truman had great respect for the United States military, but he defended vigorously the absolute supremacy of civil authority. This he did first and foremost on constitutional grounds; that is how the framers of the Constitution set up the government. But almost as important was Truman's understanding of a key difference between military and civilian administrative culture. Truman admitted that "any official," civil or military, had to rely on briefings—condensed reports and assessments from staff members. However, "the President has as his staff people of many different ideas, people who move in and out of his official family; they each have skills and professions of their own; their futures do not depend on their efficiency reports." In contrast, Truman understood that in the military, "and especially among the professionals, strong convictions and a critical mind may spell the end of a career." There is a tendency among military subordinates to please the chief by presenting briefings that reinforce what is perceived as the chief's point of view. Positives are typically stressed, whereas negatives are diminished or hidden altogether.

Truman wanted briefings that conveyed "the fullest possible range of arguments," whereas (he believed) many military leaders wanted briefings that reinforced decisions they had already arrived at.

Whether or not Truman's assessment of decision making in military culture was entirely accurate or even fair, his analysis highlights a danger all decision makers face. There is a natural human craving for affirmation and reassurance, and just as natural a tendency to avoid anything that contributes to self-doubt. The effective decision maker is burdened with trying to overcome nature. The objective of a briefing is not to find comfort or a pat on the back, but to compile facts and a variety of perspectives on those facts in order to build the best decision possible. Leaders anxious to put together staffs consisting of "team players" risk creating a corps of yes-men, a group that is not a team at all, but a monolithic monster. The members of a team work together toward common goals, but their skills are diversified. They each play a different position. Multiplication of results, not duplication of effort, is the desirable outcome of any team endeavor, and this can be achieved only by tolerating—indeed, by inviting and even requiring—a variety of takes on any given situation, problem, or opportunity. "A yes-man on the White House staff or in the Cabinet," Truman exclaimed, "is worthless!"

LESSON 109
EXPOSE DIFFERENCES OF OPINION

"I did not want fuzzy statements that concealed differences of opinions."

—*Memoirs, Volume Two: Years of Trial and Hope*

Before making any decision, President Truman "insisted on [obtaining] as complete a picture as possible." This meant hearing "all sides when there was disagreement, but even more important [it meant knowing] when disagreements existed among my advisors." Truman wanted positions stated sharply and clearly, and he did not want to hear "fuzzy statements that concealed differences of opinions."

Too often, managers and other leaders hear what they want to hear. If, consciously or unconsciously, the message is conveyed to the organization that only agreement and consensus are desirable, then only agreement and consensus will be returned, whether or not the matters at issue warrant it. In the absence of genuine consensus, members of the group will try to provide the illusion of agreement by stating conclusions in terms sufficiently fuzzy to obscure points of difference. No leader or organization profits from the willful distortion of reality.

Why do so many leaders shun disagreement? Truman suggested that differences of opinion among advisers implied inefficiency. Perhaps they do, but, as Truman went on to observe, absolute agreement "may be efficiency in military administration, but not in government at the top level." He believed, on the contrary, that "the best results come from intensive study of different viewpoints and from arguments pro and con." Besides, "efficiency" was a quality Truman always associated with dictatorships, not with creative leadership, which in the long run is far more productive than merely efficient management.

LESSON 110
FOLLOW YOUR INNER COMPASS

"I have never felt that popularity and glamour are fundamentals by which the Chief Executive of the government should operate. A President has to know where he is going and why, and he must believe in what he is doing."

—*Memoirs, Volume Two: Years of Trial and Hope*

An appetite for popularity and glamour is not a good motive for seeking leadership. "A President cannot always be popular. He has to be able to say *yes* and *no*, and more often *no* to most of the propositions that are put up to him. . . ." Pressure from the public, from special interests, and from individuals can be intense and unremitting, but "if a President is easily influenced and interested in keeping in line with the press and the polls, he is a complete washout."

Pushed and pulled a dozen different ways, you must rely on your inner compass to stay the course *you* believe in. Navigating by the whims, wishes, praise, and condemnation of others is not leadership, but something closer to pandering or, at worst, yielding to blackmail.

LESSON 111
THE ENERGY TO DECIDE

"I have never forced myself to think when my energy was low. I simply will not tackle a problem involving an important decision until I feel completely relaxed."

—Speech at Columbia University, April 28, 1959

When the body is tired or stressed, the brain, the organ of decision making, is likewise tired and stressed. Fatigue may prompt impetuous, reckless decisions, but it is even more likely to produce overly cautious, timid ones. General George S. Patton—like President Truman, a leader of great decisiveness—understood this. "Tired officers are always pessimists," he observed.

Prepare for decision making as you would prepare for an athletic event. Condition yourself. Get as much rest as you can. Free yourself from distraction. Recharge. Then act.

LESSON 112
HOLD NO COW SACRED

"The atom bomb was no 'great decision.'"

—Speech at Columbia University, April 28, 1959

In the course of a three-day lecture and seminar program at Columbia University in April 1959, former president Truman mentioned that the most difficult decision during his administration was to fight in Korea, because it "involved a world-wide policy on the part of the Free World." A student asked why Truman felt that the Korea decision "was greater than dropping the atom bomb." Truman replied that the "atom bomb was no 'great decision.' . . . It was merely another powerful weapon in the arsenal of righteousness. The dropping of the [two atomic] bombs stopped the war, saved millions of lives. It was a purely military decision."

Truman never voiced any second thoughts about his decision to use the bomb. He refused to cloud the decision-making process by according the atomic bomb any special moral or philosophical status. It was a tool, as he saw it, "merely another powerful weapon."

In evaluating a situation or making a decision, examine your assets and options as objectively as possible. Don't mystify the decision-making process with taboos or sacred cows. Try to lay everything on the table and entertain all possibilities. Ideally, all options and assets should be available for you to choose among.

If it is necessary to hold anything back, be absolutely certain that doing so confers a benefit and is not a product of habit or outworn belief.

LESSON 113
LIVE WITH YOUR DECISIONS

"I was there. I did it. I would do it again."

—Speech at Columbia University, April 28, 1959

"Mr. President," a Columbia University student asked Truman, "would you be willing to explain to us what led you to believe that the first atomic bomb had failed to achieve peace with Japan and made it necessary to drop the second one?"

Truman answered that the decision was made as "a military procedure," to destroy major manufacturing centers and thereby "shut off the supplies to the Japanese."

"The reason I asked this," the student continued, "was that it seemed to me the second bomb came pretty soon after the first one, two or three days."

Truman agreed that the second bomb was dropped soon after the first, but then remarked, perhaps somewhat impatiently: "All this uproar about what we did and what could have been stopped—should we take these wonderful Monday morning quarterbacks, the experts who are supposed to be right? They don't know what they are talking about. I was there. I did it. I would do it again."

The decisions of any leader are subject to second-guessing, especially long after the fact. It is both arrogant and foolish to close your ears to all criticism, but the viable alternative to a head in the sand is not a career of agonized self-doubt. Before you weigh the "contributions" of your critics, repeat Truman's formula: *I was there. I did it.* Whatever else they say, those Monday-morning quarterbacks can't say this. Then, given these facts, ask yourself: *Would I do it again?* If you, who were there and who did it, can answer *yes*, chances are that you made the best decision you could at that time and in your place.

LESSON 114
MAKING UP YOUR MIND

"You get all the facts and you make up your mind."

—Quoted in *Memorial Services in the Congress of the United States and Tributes in Eulogy of Harry S. Truman, Late a President of the United States*

The formal education of Harry Truman ended with graduation from high school, a little bit of business college, and a smattering of law. Had his family's economic situation been more advantageous, he would certainly have gone on to college. Indeed, Truman was an avid reader throughout his life. "I know I read the wrong books," Charles Robbins quoted him in *Last of His Kind: An Informal Portrait of Harry S. Truman*, "but I read a lot, and I suppose I got some good ones now and then."

Truman was a natural student, always hungry for the facts. Facts—not intuition, not judgment, not divine inspiration, and certainly not a roll of the dice—formed the basis of every leadership decision Truman made. "As president," he remarked in his memoirs, "I always insisted on as complete a picture as possible before making a decision, and I did not want fuzzy statements that concealed differences of opinion."

This is a sound model for any decision maker, but it is not without a pitfall, for it is all too tempting to allow the fact-finding process to delay and even displace the decision-making process: *I can't decide yet; I need more facts.* Truman avoided this by what can only be described as gritty resolve. He noted in his diary on June 15, 1952:

> [The presidency] is the greatest office in the history of the world. Not one of the great oriental potentates, Roman Emperors, French Kings, Napoleon, Victoria, Queen of Great Britain, Jenghis Khan, Tamerlane, the Mogul Emperors, the great Caliph of Baghdad had half the power and influence that the President of the United States now has. It is a terrifying responsibility. But the responsibility has to be met and the decisions made—right or wrong.

There is no secret formula here, just three truths. Truth 1: The responsibility of leadership ranges from heavy to "terrifying." Truth 2: The responsibility has to be met and the decisions made. Truth 3: *Making* the decisions is even more important than whether they are right or wrong. It is a great part of Truman's genius for leadership that he could accept these truths absolutely. Doubtless, he was helped in this by the attitude he articulated in "My First Eighty Years," an article written for the *Saturday Evening Post*, June 13, 1964: "Once I had made the decision, I didn't worry over it. If I made a wrong decision, I made another one to correct it."

For the effective leader, *doing* is always more important than *being*. Leadership is not a state but a process. The mistake that paralyzes too many would-be leaders is picturing leadership as a throne instead of what it is, a vehicle. Leadership is not for sitting. It's for moving—for pulling—for pushing. And if a decision you make turns the vehicle off course, another decision must be made to straighten it out again—and, if necessary, again and again.

LESSON 115
USE ALL AVAILABLE BRAINS

"A good president is a man who's able to use the brains and ability of all the people that he can persuade to come and advise him."

—Quoted in *Where the Buck Stops: The Personal and Private Writings of Harry S. Truman* (Margaret Truman, ed.)

No chief executive was more aware than Truman of the awful and ultimate loneliness of leadership at the highest level. As president, he understood and fully accepted that the buck stopped with him. Yet even he believed that effective leadership could never be entirely a solo act. For him, one test of a leader's effectiveness was the ability to identify, recruit, muster, and use the talent of others. While accepting responsibility for all results, a good leader effectively marshals all the intellectual resources of the organization to aid in gathering and evaluating the facts on which every major decision is based.

LESSON 116
RIDE THE ENGINE OF CRISIS

"Though this may sound like a strange thing to say, a crisis can sometimes be a good thing for the country, because some men don't seem to be able to develop leadership when there's no crisis."

—Quoted in *Where the Buck Stops: The Personal and Private Writings of Harry S. Truman* (Margaret Truman, ed.)

No leader welcomes a crisis, but even a crisis may have an upside. Crisis, Truman believed, occasioned the "best actions of many presidents" and may thus be regarded as an engine of inspiration. Of course, there is no guarantee that crisis will evoke brilliant leadership. Panic and paralysis are other possible responses. The most effective leadership strategy is to do everything possible to anticipate crisis and, what is more, to prepare not only to meet crisis, but to exploit its potential to energize the entire organization. From his predecessor, Franklin Roosevelt, Truman learned to value what FDR termed "the goad of suffering."

LESSON 117

IF YOU KEEP YOUR EAR TO THE
GROUND, HOW CAN YOU HEAR
YOURSELF THINK?

"[President Martin Van Buren] was always worrying about what might happen if he did this or that; and always keeping his ear to the ground to the point where he couldn't act as the chief executive. . . ."

—Quoted in *Where the Buck Stops: The Personal and Private Writings of Harry S. Truman* (Margaret Truman, ed.)

Truman was a great believer in talking to people and generally getting out among them, but he never considered his role as chief executive to be the proxy for the people, a passive agent of their will. Most of the presidents whom Truman condemned as "nonentities" were, in his judgment, lazy, preferring inaction to leadership. Truman considered the eighth president, Martin Van Buren, who served from 1837 to 1841, a nonentity, but he was also a special case. His besetting flaw was not laziness, but an overabundance of concern about public opinion. "I don't know whether or not he even had any personal philosophy on the role of government; I think he was a man who was always worrying about what might happen if he did this or that, and always keeping his ear to the ground. . . ." He listened so intently to the voice of the people that he could not hear his own—if, indeed, it ever dared to speak to him.

All effective leaders need to be good politicians, listening and responding to the members of the group, but being a good politician is not all there is to leadership. As Truman observed of Van

Buren, "He was just a politician and nothing more, a politician who was out of his depth." Leaders chart the course for their enterprise. They do not merely divine the will of the people and see that it is executed. If you fail to lead your enterprise, it will lead you. But to what destination or doom?

LESSON 118

THE PHASES OF DECISION

"The ability to make up your mind sounds as if it speaks for itself, but it really isn't as simple as all that."

—Quoted in *Where the Buck Stops: The Personal and Private Writings of Harry S. Truman* (Margaret Truman, ed.)

In his posthumously edited and published *Where the Buck Stops*, Truman analyzed the decision-making process, dividing it into three distinct phases.

First: A president "not only [has] to decide what's right according to the principles by which he's been raised and educated, but he also has to be willing to listen to a lot of people, all kinds of people, and find out what effect the decision he's about to make will have on the people."

There are two steps within this phase. First comes a decision based on personal judgment. As we've learned, Truman did not believe that a democratic leader was an agent of the popular will. He was the people's representative, elected to use his own best judgment for the common good. Next comes listening to the people. Note, however, that the object of such listening is not to find out what the people want. Truman based his judgment not on what the people say they want, but on what effect the action they propose will have on them. His focus was not on the collective personality of those he led, but on the effect his decision would have.

Second: The next phase of making a decision is to act: "And

when he makes up his mind that his decision is correct, he mustn't let himself be moved from that decision under any consideration. He must go through with that program and not be swayed by the pressures that are put on him by people who tell him that his decision is wrong."

This is the "secret" of "decisive people." They devote time, energy, and an abundance of thought to crafting and weighing the decision. During the first phase, they may try out several positions and consider various alternatives. However, once the decision is made, there is no looking back, second-guessing, or yielding to the pressure of naysayers and Monday-morning quarterbacks. The second phase is exclusively follow-through.

Time does not stop once a decision is made. This brings us to the third phase: "If the decision is wrong, all he has to do is get some more information and make another decision, because he's also got to have the ability to change his mind and start over." Understand this: No matter how consequential, few decisions are permanent or terminal. Leadership is a work in progress. Neither despair nor put your feet up. You've still got work to do.

CHAPTER 9

FACTS OF THE MATTER

LESSON 119
USE HISTORY

"One of my early hobbies had been investigating the part which open avenues of communication had played in the shaping of history."

—*Memoirs, Volume One: Year of Decisions*

While Truman enjoyed reading about the past, he never did so only for entertainment. He absorbed the lessons of history, and he applied them:

> I had learned from my reading that Alexander's empire fell apart at his death primarily because there was no easy access from one section of the empire to another. Rome's supremacy over such a long period of time was in large part due to her wonderful roads, some of which are still in use as arterial highways in various parts of Europe.

When he became presiding judge in Jackson County, Missouri, Truman drew on his youthful reading of ancient history and applied it to the present: "I . . . worked hard and long for a Kansas City regional plan which, among other things, would make a complete study of transportation and communication needs for the entire six-county area, and I had supervised the road-building program of Jackson County as well." Later still, when he was elected to the U.S. Senate, he used his assignment to the Interstate

Commerce Committee (in 1935) as an "opportunity to help do something about [the] pressing need" for the expansion of the national highway system and the "air transport industry."

Use everything that comes your way. Learn from the past— the ancient past, the past of others, the recent past, and your own personal past. Everything is a lesson, to be filed away in some corner of the mind for later application to some situation, problem, or opportunity.

LESSON 120
PUT YOURSELF OUT

"I got into my automobile and started out from Washington to make a little investigation on my own. I drove thirty thousand miles in a great circle through Maryland and from there down to Florida, across to Texas, north through Oklahoma to Nebraska, and back through Wisconsin and Michigan."

—*Memoirs, Volume One: Year of Decisions*

Supervisory, management, and leadership positions appeal to some people as an opportunity to put their feet up and let others do all the hard work. Truman understood that, done right, the leader's job is the hardest of all—and not just intellectually and emotionally, but physically, too. An effective leader is always putting himself out, figuratively as well as literally.

Early in 1941, when Senator Truman became aware of widespread inefficiency and waste among government defense contractors, a situation that not only was costly but also dangerously threatened the pace of preparation for war, he "decided to take a closer look at it." A "closer look" meant driving himself some 30,000 miles to visit "war camps, defense plants, and other establishments and projects which had some connection with the total war effort of the country. . . ." Truman commented that "the trip was an eye-opener, and I came back to Washington convinced that something needed to be done fast." He "had seen at first hand" that rumors circulating about inefficiency and corruption were based on fact. Using this firsthand information as his springboard, Truman called for a Senate committee to investigate the conduct of the defense program. Chaired by Truman, the committee was spectacularly successful. It identified problems and, by working with the contractors involved, solved them. The result contributed to the extraordinary pace and volume of war-materials production that were instrumental in winning World War II.

LESSON 121
DON'T DROWN IN A SEA
OF INFORMATION

"I told [Secretary of State Edward R.] Stettinius [Jr.] that I would welcome both the daily summary and the reference book, but I requested him to let me have that same day an outline of the background and the present status of the principal problems confronting this government in its relations with other countries."

—Memoirs, Volume One: Year of Decisions

When Franklin Roosevelt's death put Harry Truman in the White House, Truman understood that what he now needed was the information that would transform him from merely the new occupant of the house into the president of the United States. FDR had done virtually nothing to bring his vice president up to speed on a world situation that was as dangerous as it was complex. Truman needed to learn, and he needed to learn fast.

Secretary of State Edward R. Stettinius, Jr., informed the new president that the State Department, pursuant to FDR's orders, prepared a daily two-page summary of important diplomatic developments. Handing Truman the current report, Stettinius asked if he wanted to continue the daily reports and also offered him an up-to-date reference book. Truman enthusiastically accepted the reports and the book, but he also asked for something more: a document that would outline everything he needed to know about the international problems the government faced.

Information is capable of sustaining as well as overwhelming.

Devote effort to designing systems of information that will feed rather than choke you. Determine which categories of fact are most important and turn your mind to these. Where information is concerned, work up a "leadership diet," consuming only what you absolutely need. A big part of leadership resides in the faculty of discrimination, deciding not only what actions to put out into the world, but what data to take in.

LESSON 122
ALWAYS DEMAND THE TRUTH

"'I want the truth,' I told him, 'and I want the facts at all times. I want you to stay with me and always to tell me what's on your mind. You may not always agree with my decisions, but I know you will carry them out faithfully.'"

—To Admiral William D. Leahy, chief of staff to the commander in chief, quoted in *Memoirs, Volume One: Year of Decisions*

You're trying on a new suit. You ask your friend, "How does this look on me?" and she replies, "Do you want the truth?" Without thinking, you say, "Of course I do."

But do you? Do you really want to be told that it makes you look fat or it's a "little too youthful" for you? Do you really want the truth?

When Truman asked Leahy to stay on in his administration and continue to perform the special advisory function he had performed for FDR, the admiral responded: "Are you sure you want me, Mr. President? I always say what's on my mind."

That is when Truman said, "I want the truth."

It takes character to ask for the truth and mean it. Contradiction, bad news, and disappointment are difficult to take, but if they are part of the truth, you have to accept them or risk a destructive separation from reality. When you ask for the truth, be sure you *want* the truth, then be sincerely grateful for it, however agreeable or disagreeable it may be.

LESSON 123
THE BEST INFORMATION IS
FIRSTHAND INFORMATION

"What I now wanted from [FDR adviser Harry] Hopkins was more firsthand information about the heads of state with whom I would have to deal, particularly Stalin."

—Memoirs, Volume One: Year of Decisions

Assuming the mantle of the presidency on the death of Franklin Roosevelt, Truman immersed himself in reports and analyses. "On that first full day as President I did more reading than I ever thought I could," but, having done the reading, what he "now wanted . . . was more firsthand information." He summoned Harry Hopkins, FDR's longtime adviser, intimate friend, perennial emissary, and perpetual point man. Truman hoped to obtain from Hopkins personal insight into the character of the other leaders he now had to deal with. The president was not disappointed: "Hopkins was a storehouse of information and was rarely at a loss for a word or a fact. Furthermore, he was usually able to describe and characterize the many important figures he had met."

Information is only as good as its source. Most data go stale fast, and facts get worn, frayed, and patched as they pass from hand to hand. Put a premium on what you can obtain firsthand, the closer to the source the better. Set up, deploy, and use your listening posts. Ask questions as often as you can.

LESSON 124
ESTABLISH ROLES

"Cabinet members were simply a Board of Directors appointed by the President, to help him carry out policies of the Government. . . ."

> —Notation on White House appointment sheet,
> May 18, 1945

Do this from the very beginning: Make your role as leader a *fact* and, based on this fact, create roles for everyone else. This is a leadership act that needs to be carried out with a clarity and decisiveness that leave no unanswered questions and that is not, in any case, open to question.

At 2 P.M. on May 18, 1945, a little more than one month after assuming office following the death of FDR, Truman "Held Cabinet Meeting" and

> . . . explained to Cabinet members that in my opinion the Cabinet members were simply a Board of Directors appointed by the President, to help him carry out policies of the Government; in many instances the Cabinet could be of tremendous help to the President by offering advice whether he liked it or not but when President [gave] an order they should carry it out. I told them I expected to have a Cabinet I could depend on and take in my confidence and if this confidence

was not well placed I would get a Cabinet in which I could place confidence.

Here is an admirably clear statement of expectations:

1. The Cabinet has high responsibility, but is subordinate to the president.
2. Cabinet members are expected to advise the president and to pull no punches in so doing, "offering advice whether he liked it or not."
3. Although Cabinet members are invited to debate and disagree with the president, debate and disagreement end when an order is finally issued. From that point on, the Cabinet is to carry out the president's policy, whether *they* like it or not.
4. The president expects a Cabinet he can depend on. Failing this expectation, he will "get a Cabinet in which I could place confidence."

These are the *facts* of the relationship between President Harry S. Truman and his Cabinet, subject to neither discussion nor dispute.

LESSON 125
KNOW WHAT YOU DON'T KNOW

"Now, wouldn't it be silly for me to try to ape the language of men whose business is ships?"

—Quoted in *Merriman Smith's Book of Presidents: A White House Memoir* (Timothy Smith, ed.)

Sailing to the momentous Potsdam Conference at the end of World War II aboard the cruiser *Augusta*, Truman remarked to reporters that he was going "upstairs" to the "front porch" for a breath of air. When a reporter kidded him for calling the forecastle a front porch and for saying that he was going upstairs rather than the nautically proper "above," Truman responded that the only other time he'd been to sea was when he shipped out to France during World War I and returned. He asked the reporter: "Now, wouldn't it be silly for me to try to ape the language of men whose business is ships?"

It is important for a leader to know what he knows, and it is just as important for him to know what he doesn't know. Remembering a store of facts is not real knowledge. Awareness of the limits of that store is a necessary dimension of true knowledge. As far as taking action is concerned—and that is the ultimate business of a leader—mere facts are useless. Intelligent decisions require knowing what you know as well as what you don't know. It is a threadbare strategy indeed to lead by continually faking it.

LESSON 126

READ THE FINE PRINT

"Nearly every memorandum has a catch in it and it has been necessary to read at least a thousand of 'em and as many reports."

—Diary entry, June 1, 1945

Micromanager became a dirty word in business circles, especially during the 1980s, the "Reagan years," when that genial chief executive was celebrated as a "big-picture guy," who smilingly delegated one responsibility after another in a resolute refusal to "get bogged down" in details.

The word *micromanagement* was unknown to Truman and his era, but he wouldn't have been afraid of the accusation. Like any effective leader, Truman delegated tasks and responsibilities—as one must in managing a complex organization—but he monitored operations and results with apparently tireless vigilance. He believed, as he once wrote to his daughter, that "95 percent of people are honest," but he never forgot the remaining 5 percent. And even honest people make mistakes or, at the very least, differ in their interpretations of the same set of circumstances.

"Have been going through some very hectic days," the president noted in his diary on June 1, 1945. "Eyes troubling somewhat. Too much reading 'fine print.' Nearly every memorandum has a catch in it and it has been necessary to read at least a thousand of 'em and as many reports."

Is micromanagement a leadership error? Yes, it is. But so is an exclusive focus on the big picture. If it is dangerous to fail to see the forest for the trees, it can be equally catastrophic to ignore the trees by gazing at the forest. Never forget that the big picture consists of details and that the connection between them is seamless. This being the case, commit yourself to a workday that is both intellectually challenging and physically demanding. Fine print and sore eyes are part of the job.

LESSON 127

GATHER—AND USE—THE FACTS

"That is my hardest decision to date. But I'll make it when I have all the facts."

—Diary entry, June 17, 1945

Reading any bare-bones summary of World War II, it all seems pretty simple: Two atomic attacks, against Hiroshima and Nagasaki, abruptly ended the war with Japan. But in the weeks and months following the death of Franklin Roosevelt, the situation was anything but simple. Truman soon learned of the existence of the atomic bomb program, called the Manhattan Project, and knew that it was approaching culmination. At the time, however, no one knew whether "the gadget" (as, for security reasons, the new weapon was called) would prove an effective military weapon or even if it would work at all. Truman understood that it might well be sufficiently destructive to bring about an end to the war, but until that actually happened, he had to operate under the assumption that the Japanese, who had been consistently suicidal in their resistance, would fight to the end. Without the atomic bomb, two endgame strategies were in the offing, both costly in Allied and Japanese lives. As Truman noted in his diary: "I have to decide Japanese strategy—shall we invade Japan proper or shall we bomb [with conventional munitions] and blockade?"

It was a decision of the most terrible proportions. To bomb and blockade would likely prolong the war, but according to planners, an invasion that might shorten the war would cost half a million Allied casualties.

"That is my hardest decision to date," Truman noted. What would his next words be? "How can I possibly decide?" or "What am I to do?" or "Why me?" No. He wrote a simple declarative statement: "But I'll make it when I have all the facts."

Facts enable a decision. They do not guarantee the rightness of the decision, but no leader, no matter how bold or talented, can be expected to create something from nothing, to fashion a decision out of thin air. Climb to your decision on a mountain of facts.

LESSON 128
PLAY CHESS, NOT CHECKERS

"At the same time I asked [my Cabinet and advisers] to consider carefully places where trouble might break out. What, for instance, would Mao Tse-tung do? What might the Russians do in the Balkans, in Iran, in Germany?"

—*Memoirs, Volume Two: Years of Trial and Hope*

In the years after he left the White House, Truman was inevitably and repeatedly asked some version of *What was your hardest decision?* And just as inevitably, people were surprised by his answer. It was never "the decision to drop the atom bomb." Invariably, he would utter a single word: *Korea.*

When Communist North Korea invaded the democratic South in 1950, Truman had to decide whether to intervene, how to intervene, and to what extent to intervene. His goal, as always, was to contain the expansion of communism without igniting a third world war. If fighting an all-out war is devastatingly difficult, fighting a "limited war" is even harder. The president had to weigh each enlargement of the war effort with the greatest of care. How far could he push before provoking the Chinese or the Soviets to worldwide battle?

Truman understood that he had to play chess, not checkers. Concentrating on the local effect of any given move would have been a woefully inadequate strategy. He needed to assess the remote consequences of everything he proposed to do—consequences that were remote in place as well as in time. He asked his

Cabinet, the chiefs of staff, and other advisers to consider what effects expanding the war would have, not just on the Korean situation, but in various "places where trouble might break out." Would Mao intervene in Korea? What would the Soviets do in such contested and far-flung places as the Balkans, Iran, and Germany?

Effective leadership often requires thinking in multiple dimensions. No one expects you to be a psychic, to see things that are far away in place and time, but you should possess sufficient wit to *imagine* the plausible scenarios that might develop as a result of any particular action. A decent devotee of checkers pounces on the chance to jump an opponent's piece whenever and wherever the opportunity presents itself. A seasoned chess player, in contrast, endeavors to look through each move, envisioning how it will play out two, three, six moves down the line. In an organization of even rudimentary complexity, each decision has consequences more or less remote from the immediate sphere of that decision. Move like a chess player, always contemplating the moves that this move will provoke, the many moves that likely lie ahead.

LESSON 129
NEVER GET CLOSE TO A SKUNK

"Nobody, not even the president of the United States, can approach too close to a skunk, in skunk territory, and expect to get anything out of it except a bad smell."

—Quoted in John Hersey, *Aspects of the Presidency*

Few public officials were more frank in their disapproval of Joseph McCarthy, the Red-baiting senator from Wisconsin, than Harry S. Truman. "I recognized him immediately as a fake and a phony," he wrote in a manuscript published after his death, "and a real menace to our country and our principles of freedom and decency. . . . And I let my staff and the Congress and the rest of the world know how I felt about McCarthy every chance I got" (Margaret Truman, ed., *Where the Buck Stops: The Personal and Private Writings of Harry S. Truman*). However, when Truman met privately with advisers to discuss ways of countering McCarthy and McCarthyism, he flatly rejected the suggestion of one aide that the administration make public a dossier detailing McCarthy's sexual escapades.

"You must not ask the president of the United States to get down in the gutter with a guttersnipe," Truman replied. "Nobody, not even the president of the United States, can approach too close to a skunk, in skunk territory, and expect to get anything out of it except a bad smell."

Truman knew that you cannot sling mud without getting muddy, and he understood that he could not allow the office he held to become tainted. To do so would compromise his authority and, even worse, permanently diminish the office of president of the United States. To remain effective, a leader cannot afford to use improper or unseemly methods to defeat the opposition, even if—indeed, *especially* if—these are the methods of the opposition itself. To remain effective, a leader must ultimately stand above the fray. He cannot roll around in the mud.

What, then, was the proper prescription against McCarthy?

"If you think somebody is telling a big lie about you," Truman told his advisers, "the only way to answer is with the whole truth."

In the end, rely on facts. Let these defeat the opposition. Rely on the truth presented frankly and fully to the members of the organization. When Truman gave a series of talks and seminars at Columbia University in 1959, he was asked by Lindsay Rogers, a professor of public law, if he thought television helped expose McCarthy for what he was and "helped to shorten the hysteria period." Truman responded: "I sure do. When they saw him on television they found out exactly what he was." And Truman added, with typical good humor: "You better be careful when you get on that television, too."

LESSON 131
BE *TRULY* CONSERVATIVE

"It is my opinion that any Senator of the United States who wants to abolish the Constitution and create a Confederacy is a dangerous citizen and should be checked and balanced so he cannot accomplish his purpose."

—Letter to Senator Thomas C. Hennings, Jr., March 25, 1955

Three years after leaving the White House, Harry Truman continued to defend the office of president of the United States and, in doing so, revealed himself as an example of true conservatism. Now, Harry Truman was called a lot of things, both during and after his career, but *conservative* was not a label customarily applied to him. Indeed, as Truman saw it, conservatism, as practiced by most of his Republican colleagues and opponents, was nothing more than a defense of the status quo for the perceived further enrichment of the wealthy and established and at the expense of the working class and the struggling. The essence of conservatism, as he saw it, was inaction and, therefore, the antithesis of leadership.

Yet Truman was a conservative, by no means in the conventionally understood political sense, but in his philosophical approach to statecraft. An example is the letter he wrote to Thomas C. Hennings, Jr., a member of the Senate Committee on the Judiciary, concerning a proposed amendment to the Constitution introduced by Senator John W. Bricker of Ohio to severely limit the president's power to make treaties. In his letter, Truman pointed out that Article II of the Constitution already provided for ratification of all treaties by a vote of two-thirds of the Senate. "If the powers of the President are further limited by amendment as suggested, the country may as well readopt the [notoriously weak and ineffective] Articles of Confederation and go back to a Greek city state."

This is the beginning of Truman's historical argument against the proposed amendment. In effect, he said, it has been tried before. Under the Articles of Confederation, which were adopted during the Revolution, there was no chief executive, Congress had little authority, and all real power rested with the individual states, which were "united" not into a genuine nation, but in a loose confederation. Shortly after the Revolution, the Articles were jettisoned in favor of the Constitution.

So much for the first part of the historical argument against the proposed amendment: *Been there, done that.* In his second point, Truman got to the heart of his historical argument: "The men who wrote the Constitution knew history, were familiar with government as practiced in their day and had become experienced in the shortcomings of the Articles of Confederation." The Constitution was based on a knowledge of history and a thorough experience of the present, Truman argued. The implications of this statement are profound. No document like the United States Constitution had ever been written before. In this sense, it was innovative, even radical. And yet, Truman argued in his letter, it was also conservative in that it refused to discard history or the collective experience of the present. It built on the past and on the present, including knowledge of other governments and the experience of government under the Articles of Confederation. The Bricker Amendment, in contrast, proposed by a so-called conservative Republican, was the worst kind of radicalism in that it would simply discard history and experience. Whatever Bricker was politically, the proposed amendment revealed him as the opposite of conservative in philosophy. As Truman saw it, *radical* was not the appropriate word for what Bricker proposed. In this case, *wasteful* was the better antonym of *conservative*, because Bricker would not so much change or transform a cornerstone of American government as throw it away.

Truman concluded his letter by stating, "It required eighty years of experience, a John Marshall and a Civil War to establish and confirm the greatest document of government in the history of the world."

No leader worth the name gives knee-jerk support to the status quo. As Truman saw it, the only worthwhile leader was an activist, who made it his business to identify needs and then to lead those who would implement the means of addressing them, who identified problems and marshaled the resources to solve them, who defined objectives and focused the energies of the organization on attaining them. This did not require an arbitrary break with the past. On the contrary, the most effective way of leading into the future was to build on the experience of the past. Guide the enterprise into the future while rigorously, even reverently, conserving what is best and most useful from the past. A mindless adherence to the status quo is paralysis, but a thoughtless break with the past is waste as obscene as it is dangerous, and "any Senator . . . who wants to abolish the Constitution and create a Confederacy is a dangerous citizen and should be checked and balanced so he cannot accomplish his purpose."

LESSON 132
MAKE A CONTRACT OF FACT

"I'm going to answer some questions for you, if I can. If I can't, why then we'll go and look them up and I'll answer them tomorrow."

—Speech at Columbia University, April 27, 1959

The Old Testament King Solomon is an archetype of the wise leader, the ruler second only to God in his omniscience. Even in the modern world, we expect our leaders to have the answers—at least most of them. More often than not, of course, this expectation is unrealistic. However, an effective leader must make a contract with those he leads not necessarily to *know* all the answers, but always to endeavor to find them, to gather the facts in pursuit of the truth no matter where they may lead.

To the students and professors in his Columbia University audience, Truman did not promise more than he could deliver. He would answer what questions he could. But he did not allow his modesty to breach the unwritten contract he made with this audience. If he couldn't answer some questions today, he'd "look them up and . . . answer them tomorrow."

249

LESSON 133

FOLLOW THE SHOW, NOT THE TELL

"Budget figures reveal far more about proposed policy than speeches."

—Quoted in Dean Acheson, *Present at the Creation: My Years in the State Department*

A leader listens, but, even more, she looks. She sees for herself. "People vote with their feet," the old saying goes. Regardless of what they may say, people walk toward what they like and away from what they don't like. They also vote with their purses, allocating funds for what they want and withholding them from what they don't want—again, regardless of what they may or may not say.

Policy, whether of government or any other organization, is surrounded by a scaffolding of words, but it is the structure within that finally counts, and that is built of resources, which by definition are always scarce. There is never enough money to do everything everyone wants every time. How these scarce resources are allocated reveals the values—the policy—of the organization, rhetoric notwithstanding.

Understand people and organizations in part by what they say, but even more by what they do: by the choices they actually make and the resources they are prepared to sacrifice to implement those choices. True policy is choice backed by sacrifice.

LESSON 134
READ TO LEAD

"Not all readers become leaders. But all leaders must be readers."

—*The Autobiography of Harry S. Truman*
(Robert H. Ferrell, ed.)

"There is nothing new in the world except the history you do not know," Harry Truman observed (William Hillman, *Mr. President*). It is especially important for a world leader, therefore, to know as much history as possible, and that means reading. But it is not only world leaders who need to do their reading. A leader needs to know the "history" relevant to whatever enterprise he or she leads. If your business is selling soap, that means devouring whatever literature you can find on the subject of making soap and selling soap, as well as the general topic of cleanliness and the related fields of shampoos, perfumes and colognes, deodorants, toothpastes, towels, baths, and showers. Get the facts. Master what is known in your industry and the markets relating to your industry. Ignorance is the enemy of leadership.

LESSON 135
OPEN YOUR MIND

"The president has to have an open mind."

—Quoted in *Where the Buck Stops: The Personal and Private Writings of Harry S. Truman* (Margaret Truman, ed.)

The president, Truman wrote in *Where the Buck Stops*, "has to get all the information he can possibly get, some of it difficult to obtain, the truthful facts behind a condition that's before him." How was he to obtain the hard-to-get facts? By a willingness "to listen to all the ideas of the people in whom he has confidence." And Truman made it his business to gather such people around him. In this he followed the example of his very favorite president, Andrew Jackson, the first chief executive to assemble a so-called kitchen cabinet to supplement his officially appointed Cabinet.

A "kitchen cabinet" is nothing more than a group of trusted advisers with whom the leader can confer confidentially, frankly, and off the record. They have no legal authority whatsoever, but they enjoy (as Truman pointed out) one privilege denied the president and his formal Cabinet. They are "people outside the publicity and the limelight that shines on the White House." This enables them to "give the president information he needs very badly without ever stopping to think about themselves."

Truman thought a kitchen cabinet was "absolutely essential," which is reason enough for any leader to consider a role for informal advisers who are responsible to him or her exclusively. If there is a downside to a kitchen cabinet it is the possibility of creating distrust and envy among those who perceive themselves as having been left out of the loop. At their most extreme, such negative sentiments may reach the level of institutional paranoia and become quite destructive. This consequence can be largely avoided, however, by taking steps to ensure the disinterested objectivity of the kitchen cabinet. Occupying a place within the inner circle must carry no special rewards, and it might even be best for the leader to draw on carefully selected outsiders for the kitchen cabinet, people who have no direct or special interest in the organization.

CHAPTER 10

DO THE RIGHT THING

LESSON 136
DON'T DO BUSINESS THAT WAY

"I don't do business that way."

—Reply of county judge Harry Truman to an offer of free
automobile seat covers in exchange for county contracts,
quoted in David McCullough, *Truman*

Ethical conduct is a daily matter. Managers and other leaders are
presented with numerous opportunities to cut corners. An ethical
leader does not evaluate each of these temptations in terms of the
magnitude of their impact, choosing, for example, to accept free
automotive upholstery (*Where's the real harm?*) but flatly rejecting
an outright bribe. Instead, he regards all temptations, minor or
major, as opportunities for doing the right thing and therefore
does the right thing rather than yield even to apparently harmless
temptation.

Ethical behavior must be practiced, literally practiced, and
then it becomes second nature, a comfortable way of doing business.

Truman, incidentally, did not lecture the automotive upholsterer about his offer. Instead, he quietly made his reply, and he
promptly paid his bill.

LESSON 137
KNOW WHEN TO BEND

". . . did not want to upset the apple cart."

—Notation on White House appointment sheet,
May 18, 1945

The Reverend Paul J. McNally, vice president of Washington's prestigious Georgetown University, called on President Truman in the Oval Office to invite him to attend commencement ceremonies and to receive an honorary degree. On the White House appointment sheet, Truman noted that he turned him down "because I have had at least 100 invitations to attend graduation exercises and have honorary degrees given me."

> Told him I am not very strong for honorary degrees if you have not earned them. I only have one and that was given or conferred on me by a little College out in Iowa, when I went out to make address to Graduating Class. Did not know they were going to confer a degree on me or would not have been there—it was too late when I found out about it not to let them go ahead with their plan—did not want to upset the apple cart.

Truman was a leader of principle, but he also knew, as all effective leaders know, when to bend. As Truman judged it, the harm of offending the students and faculty of the little college in

Iowa—upsetting their apple cart—outweighed any personal policy of refusing unearned degrees. Under some circumstances, holding fast to absolute principle is hurtfully rigid and just plain rude.

LESSON 138
MARRY REALISM TO IDEALISM

"The plan was realistic as well as idealistic."

—*Memoirs, Volume Two: Years of Trial and Hope*

As the Marshall Plan helped rebuild postwar Europe, another, more modest program, known as Point Four, was proposed by the Truman administration to aid in the economic development of regions of the Middle East, India, North Africa, and South America. Point Four would provide "technical assistance" directly to people in these underdeveloped areas to help them develop their own resources—in short, to help them help themselves. Like the Marshall Plan, Point Four was aimed at encouraging political and trade relations with the West, thereby helping to contain the expansion of communism in what came to be called the Third World.

The special beauty of the plan, as Truman saw it, was that it combined realism with idealism, qualities too easily thought of as mutually exclusive. As Truman explained, "Common sense told me that the development of these countries would keep our own industrial plant in business for untold generations. The resources of such areas as Mesopotamia, Iran, India, North Africa, and huge sections of South America have hardly been touched, and their development would be as beneficial to American trade as to the areas themselves. It would enable the peoples of many areas to subsist on trade and not aid."

"Practical" leadership does not require abandonment of idealism. Indeed, a realistic vision is invaluable in leading the implementation of even the most idealistic of projects, and idealism animates and energizes the most practical of endeavors. A worthy goal of enlightened leadership is to break down the artificial barrier dividing idealism from realism and, in fact, to join these two qualities wherever possible. As Truman observed: "The running of government is, of course, a highly practical matter. You do not operate somewhere in a theoretical heaven, but with a tough set of tough situations that have to be met—and met without hesitation. It takes practical men to run a government. But they should be practical men with a deep sense of appreciation for the higher values that the government should serve."

LESSON 139
NEVER TRADE PRINCIPLES FOR VOTES

"I have never traded principles for votes, and I did not intend to start the practice in 1948 regardless of how it might affect the election."

—Memoirs, Volume Two: Years of Trial and Hope

Thanks in large measure to party leader Harry S. Truman, the Democratic Party ran in 1948 on a platform that included a strong civil rights plank. It was the first party since Reconstruction to take such a stand, but the civil rights issue split the Democrats along the North–South axis. Those who remained the staunchest segregationists broke away as the so-called Dixiecrats and fielded South Carolina's Strom Thurmond as their candidate for president. With Republican Thomas E. Dewey a strong contender, the last thing candidate Truman needed was a split in the Democratic vote. "I knew," he later wrote, "that if I deserted the civil-liberties plank of the Democratic party platform I could heal the breach." However, Truman never seriously considered trading "principles for votes." He well understood the potential cost of his choice: "I was willing to take the risk imposed on my chances of being elected President in my own right."

Making what one knows are the right choices is not a complex process, but it can be a difficult one. However hard the choice may seem at the moment, it is helpful to bear in mind that trading enduring values for temporary gains is never a good bargain—for yourself or for the organization you lead.

LESSON 140
TRY—AND MAYBE FAIL—
FOR A GOOD CAUSE

"I am going to try to remedy it and if that ends up in my failure to be reelected, that failure will be in a good cause."

—Letter to Ernest W. Roberts, August 18, 1948

Ernie Roberts had served under "Captain Harry" in Battery D, 129th Field Artillery, during World War I. The two remained friends, and in the summer of 1948 Roberts wrote to Truman and asked him—as a fellow Southerner—to soft-pedal the civil rights issue, especially in this campaign year. Truman replied gently but firmly: "I am going to send you a copy of the report of my Commission on Civil Rights and then if you still have that antebellum proslavery outlook, I'll be thoroughly disappointed in you." He went on to cite some specific events:

> When the mob gangs can take four people out and shoot them in the back, and everybody in the country is acquainted with who did the shooting and nothing is done about it, that country is in a pretty bad fix from a law enforcement standpoint.
>
> When a Mayor and a City Marshal can take a negro [U.S. Army] Sergeant off a bus in Carolina, beat him up and put out one of his eyes, and nothing is done about it by the State Authorities, something is radically wrong with the system.
>
> On the Louisiana and Arkansas Railway when coal

burning locomotives were used, the negro firemen were the thing because it was a backbreaking job and a dirty one. As soon as they turned to oil as a fuel it became customary for people to take shots at the negro firemen and a number were murdered because it was thought that this was now a white-collar job and should go to a white man. I can't approve of such goings on and I shall never approve it, as long as I am here, as I told you before.

With this, Truman laid himself on the line: "I am going to try to remedy it and if that ends up in my failure to be reelected, that failure will be in a good cause." Yet, having staked his neck on doing the right thing, Truman refused to cast himself in a position of superiority. A good leader does the right thing. A great leader makes it possible for others to do so as well: "I know you haven't thought this thing through and that you do not know the facts." Truman concluded his letter by adding, "I am happy, however, that you wrote me because it gives me a chance to tell you what the facts are."

LESSON 141
RUN ON WHAT'S RIGHT

"It was not an encouraging situation that confronted me, but I was not brought up to run away from a fight when the fight is for what is right. Supposedly scientific predictions that I could not win did not worry me one bit."

—*Memoirs, Volume Two: Years of Trial and Hope*

Truman's 1948 campaign for election to the presidency in his own right is regarded as a classic instance of the triumph of the underdog in defiance of all odds and all pollsters. The only person who seemed not to have been surprised by his victory was Truman himself. His confidence was born not of vanity or complacence, but of a belief that he was fighting for what was right, and his success is striking evidence of the power of conviction. You can learn many things about management, about negotiation, about eloquence, and about the nitty-gritty of the enterprise you aspire to lead. But what you cannot simply acquire through study is the fire in the belly that is the conviction of the value of what you stand for and have to offer others. This you must feel and feel deeply, and it is a most powerful force.

LESSON 142
CONSIDER PRAYER

"Help me. . . ."

—Diary entry, August 15, 1950

Harry Truman was a religious man, who (onlookers noted) unabashedly kissed the Bible when he took the oath of office as president, both in 1945 and in 1949. You don't have to be religious to understand and appreciate the "prayer I said over & over all my life from eighteen years old and younger." In fact, you don't even have to believe in God to *want* the things Truman, as a leader, prayed for:

> Help me to be, to think, to act what is right, because it is right; make me truthful, honest, and honorable in all things; make me intellectually honest, for the sake of right and honor and without thought of reward to me. Give me the ability to be charitable, forgiving, and patient with my fellowmen—help me to understand their motives and their shortcomings—even as Thou understandest mine!
> Amen, Amen, Amen.

LESSON 143
WRITE YOUR OWN JOB DESCRIPTION

"But if we have [a president] who tries to do what is right because it is right, the greatest Republic in the history of the world will survive."

—Diary entry, February 18, 1952

On February 18, 1952, Harry Truman put pen to paper and drew up a list of "The President's Duties."

1. By the Constitution, he is the Executive of the Government.
2. By the Constitution, he is the Commander in Chief of the Armed Forces.
3. By the Constitution, he is the responsible head of Foreign Policy and with the help of his Secretary of State implements Foreign Policy.
4. He is the leader of his Party, makes and carries out the Party Platform as best he can.
5. He is the Social Head of the State. He entertains visiting Heads of State.
6. He is the No. 1 public relations man of the Government. He spends a lot of time persuading people to do what they should do without persuasion.
7. He has more duties and powers than a Roman Emperor, a Gen., a Hitler or a Mussolini; but he never uses those powers or prerogatives, because he is a

democrat (with a little *d*) and because he believes in
the Magna Carta and the Bill of Rights. But first he
believes in the XXth Chapter of Exodus, the Vth
Chapter of Deuteronomy, and the V, VI, & VIIth
chapters of the Gospel according to St. Matthew.

8. He should be a Cincinnatus, Marcus Aurelius An-
toninus, a Cato, Washington, Jefferson and Jackson
all in one. I fear that there is no such man. But if
we have one who tries to do what is right because it
is right, the greatest Republic in the history of the
world will survive.

Truman required great qualities in a leader and enumerated formidable duties for the president, but above all else was the resolve
to try "to do what is right because it is right." That is the cardinal
duty of leadership.

LESSON 144
EMBRACE SERVICE

"A great politician is known for the service he renders."

—Memorandum, July 1954

Americans have long been cynical about many of their leaders, so much so that *politician* has become a dirty word. Fully aware of this, Truman nevertheless always proclaimed pride in being a politician and being called a politician. Less than two years after he left the White House, he set down in a personal memorandum his criteria for a successful politician:

> It takes a life time of the hardest kind of work and study to become a successful politician. A great doctor is known by the size of his practice and his ability as a diagnostician. A great lawyer is known by his knowledge of the law and his ability to win cases and properly advise his clients. A great financier is known by the money he controls.
>
> A great politician is known for the service he renders. He does not have to become President or Governor or the head of his city or county to be a great politician. There are mayors of villages, county attorneys, county commissioners or supervisors who render just as great service locally as do the heads of the government.
>
> No young man should go into politics if he wants

to get rich or if he expects an adequate reward for his services. An honest public servant can't become rich in politics. He can only attain greatness and satisfaction by service.

Service is the essence of all effective leadership. Looked at linguistically, this may seem a paradox. For *service* shares its linguistic root with *servant*, which would seem at the very opposite end of the spectrum from *leader*. Great leaders, like Truman, either refuse to recognize any such paradox or are simply undisturbed by it. For them, *leadership* and *service* are synonymous.

LESSON 145
DEFINE "REASONABLE COMPROMISE"

"There are many issues that cannot be resolved by the surrender of either side but only through a reasonable compromise which does not sacrifice principles."

—Memoirs, Volume One: Year of Decisions

Mature leaders learn to think beyond zero-sum negotiating scenarios in which one side must win and the other must lose. "I have always felt that it does not help to keep a running box score on international events," Truman wrote. "Nor do I think it is ever helpful to have the newspapers shout 'Failure!' when our diplomatic discussions do not result in the full retreat of other nations." Many issues, Truman understood, "cannot be resolved by the surrender of either side but only through a reasonable compromise which does not sacrifice principles." Just what is a "reasonable compromise"? Truman defined it as one that "does not sacrifice principles."

Negotiating on behalf of the organization requires a firm understanding of the core principles essential to the enterprise and an equally firm resolve to adhere to these principles. Yet it also requires an understanding that these principles bracket a certain range of acceptable positions and outcomes. Make yourself thoroughly familiar with the territory that lies within those brackets, and be prepared to move within that region, which is the ground of a reasonable compromise.

LESSON 146
PRACTICE REPRESENTATIVE LEADERSHIP

"He ought to vote on what he thinks right. It's representative government."

—Seminar on Statecraft, Columbia University, April 28, 1959

A Columbia University student asked the former president whether an elected official "should vote on his own moral decisions, or . . . for what he believes his constituents want." Truman replied without hesitation: "He ought to vote on what he thinks right. It's representative government." An elected official needs to "get the facts and make up his mind on what he thinks is right. And that's the way he ought to vote." As Truman explained it, representative government is not about serving as the people's proxy, but about representing their best interests. This requires the representative to exercise his own moral and intellectual judgment and act on it. To do otherwise, to base decisions exclusively on "what he believes his constituents want," is to become, Truman said, "a demagogue."

Effective leadership is "representative government" in precisely the sense Truman defines. It is not automatically and always expressing the will of the members of the organization. At the very least, this is following, not leading; at the worst, it is dangerous demagoguery. What the representative leader "represents" is his considered judgment of the best, most ethical, most productive course for the organization, even if this judgment runs contrary in some or all respects to the consensus of the members of the organization.

In the long run, the validity of the representative leader's judgments will be either affirmed or confuted by results. Moreover, if his judgments are consistently at odds with those of the members of the organization, either he will find himself out of a job or the organization will tend to dissolve. Nobody said that leadership was a penny-ante game. But the alternative—demagoguery, leadership as "followship"—is far more destructive. It may gain the leader a short-term illusion of security, but it is really an absence of leadership, and without a leader, the organization will inevitably drift. Since drift almost always brings disaster, it is meaningless to speak of the "long-term" consequences of absent leadership. For an organization adrift, there *is* no long term.

LESSON 147
MORAL FORMULA

"If I think it is right, I am going to do it."

—Quoted in *The Harry S. Truman Encyclopedia*
(Richard S. Kirkendall, ed.)

Few equations are more straightforward than Einstein's $E = mc^2$, but none is more complex or profound in implication. So it is with Truman's apparently simple formulation "If I think it is right, I am going to do it." This is a lot more difficult than it looks. It requires, first, the confidence to believe that you are capable of judging what is right. As if this weren't demanding enough, it requires taking action on that judgment. Here is ethical leadership in the proverbial nutshell, and it requires that you ask two questions:

1. Am I confident that what I think is right is right?
2. Am I prepared to do what I think is right?

Like Truman, you must answer both in one syllable: *Yes.*

LESSON 148
AVOID THE ABYSS OF
GOOD INTENTIONS

"About the meanest thing you can say about a man [is] that he means well."

—Quoted in Ralph Keyes, *The Wit and Wisdom of Harry Truman*

When the United States entered World War I in April 1917, Harry Truman, well beyond draft age at thirty-three, volunteered. As a member of the Missouri National Guard, he had some experience in artillery, and it was as a captain of artillery that he served in France for the last three months of the war. He was serious about his military profession, serious about how he led his men and looked out for their welfare, but also serious about the business of the artillerist. It is a business, first and foremost, of deciding what to aim at, and then it is a business of taking aim and firing. The three phases of the artillery business are of equal importance. To say of an artillerist that he didn't know what to aim at would be a very bad thing to say about him; however, it might be even worse to say that he never hit what he aimed at. He meant well, but . . .

Good intentions present a paradox. While valuable, they are in and of themselves without any value at all. The value of good intentions is realized only if they are successfully acted upon. That means knowing your own intentions, working out a way to realize them in the world, then carrying through with the actions necessary to that realization. Identify the target, aim, and fire.

CHAPTER 11

USE THE BEST PART
OF THE DAY

LESSON 149
BE A MORNING PERSON

"Most people don't know when the best part of the day is: it's the early morning."

—Quoted in John Hersey, *Aspects of the Presidency*

Harry Truman spent at least part of his life as a farmer and never lost the habit of rising early—around 5 or 5:30. Like another homespun, practical American philosopher, Henry David Thoreau, Truman knew the infinite value of the morning. Thoreau ended his 1854 masterpiece, *Walden*, this way: "Only that day dawns to which we are awake. There is more day to dawn. The sun is but a morning star."

As both Thoreau and Truman knew, the morning is promise and possibility. This is half of what's needed to get things done. The other half is the necessity of meeting the day awake and ready, with high energy and high expectation. Night may be the time for dreams, but morning is the time in which dreams may be set on a course to becoming reality.

The morning mind is wide-awake and fresh, unclouded by prejudice, willing to recognize the day as something new, and able to engage that new day with vigorous imagination. Truman did much of his reading in the morning, because (he believed) that is when the mind is most receptive to new ideas. It is the time when we are closest to our most original selves and when we can be most confident that our thoughts and feelings are truly our own. Morning is a time of preparation for decisions that will result in action.

LESSON 150
SOMETIMES YOU HAVE TO
CLOSE YOUR DOOR

"It seems to me that we have seen enough visiting firemen and potential promoters and chiselers."

—Memo to Matthew Connelly, Truman's appointments secretary, September 1945

Truman habitually scribbled comments on his daily appointment sheets. For example:

SEPTEMBER 21, 1945

12:30 [group of three professional educators]
Gave me a great song & dance on education.
12:45 Dorothy K. Roosevelt, Diana Roosevelt
Just came in. Don't know why.

SEPTEMBER 26, 1945

11:30 Ely Culbertson [bridge player]
Has a way to save the world, but I doubt its efficacy.
11:45 Chester Gray [farmers' association representative]
An old baloney peddler.

And so on.

Truman believed it extremely important to be accessible to those with a genuine need to see him, but not every need was genuine. As powerful as the president or any leader may be, he is in one respect impoverished. His resources of time are extremely limited. Realizing this, and deciding he was being burdened by too many "visiting firemen," Truman acted to limit his callers.

If it is important to see people who have a genuine need, it is equally important to qualify "genuine need." For Truman, the qualifying question was this: Will seeing this visitor benefit the nation? If the answer was no, there was a very good chance that the president's door would remain closed.

Managing time is in large part managing people, and that begins with deciding which people, in a given situation, truly need some of your very limited supply of minutes, a resource that is entirely nonrenewable.

LESSON 151
MANAGE YOUR TIME

"It seems there's somebody for supper every night."

—Quoted in *Merriman Smith's Book of Presidents:
A White House Memoir* (Timothy Smith, ed.)

To lead people, you must first manage time. President Truman recorded a typical workday in a diary entry of February 20, 1952:

> Was up at 5:40 A.M. Shaved and dressed by 6:05. Listened to a news broadcast at 5:55 and at 6:10 was reading documents by the wholesale—so many of them and so much "fine print" I missed my 7 o'clock walk.
>
> The "Boss" [Mrs. Truman] and I had breakfast at 8:30 and about 8:50 I went to the White House office. . . .
>
> Begin to dictate answers to my personal mail, to my dictation secretary. When that is done I sit for an artist who is making a model for a medallion. But I read documents all the time too.
>
> Then I send for the Chief Clerk of the White House and sign whatever documents have accumulated. Sign on an average 600 a day, 365 days in the year. It is 10 o'clock by now and I call in the staff. The press secretary tells me what he expects to be asked at

his 10:30 press reception, gives me articles and editorials to read.

The Assistant to the President then gives me the results of Senatorial and Congressional interviews and requests; tells me what the boards and bureaus are doing and makes recommendations for decisions.

The Appointment Secretary submits requests for appointments and recommendations as to which ones should come to see me. He hands [me] the invitations to make speeches and public appearances and the whole staff takes part in the discussion.

The Legal Counselor to the President discusses interviews with the Atty. Gen. Counselors of the Depts. suggest the signing or rejection of executive orders, discuss the legal aspects of legislation etc.

The executive assistants report one at a time on special matters, appointments to office, disgruntled minority groups, labor problems and whatever else needs the attention of the President.

The able correspondence Secretary makes suggestions on messages to be sent to various meetings over the country, birthdays and special days to be remembered and remarked. . . .

Then the Army Aide is consulted. He reports on selective service medals and citations, complaints of mammas, court martials, etc. The Naval and Air Aides follow the same procedure. . . .

The Chief Clerk presents more documents and papers to be signed.

Soon as the staff is dismissed the Intelligence service reports what goes on all around the world. . . .

Then comes the appointment list, Senators, Congressmen, visiting preachers, prize winners, Cabinet members and anyone else who can get by the Appointment Secretary. There is from one to forty every fifteen minutes until 1 P.M. Then a lunch, a thirty minute nap, and at 3 P.M. more appointments, maybe a press conference, sometimes a session in the White House pool—but not often—then . . . across the street [to Blair House, where the president and his family lived during extensive renovation of the White House] to spend the evening on papers getting ready for another day.

It really is a great life—if you like it!

While the president's workload was heavy, he managed it so that it was never overwhelming. His routine, while not rigid, was clear; with the assistance of his staff, he always attempted to slot the work into a prescribed schedule.

Except in the case of emergencies, which make their own schedules, it is a mistake to allow immediate circumstances to dictate the structure of the workday. Indeed, doing so results in a day that is not structured at all. Intelligent time management requires adhering to a schedule, for yielding in this way ultimately puts the executive in control of the day, whereas abandoning the structure of a schedule puts the leader and the organization at the mercy of the day and whatever it may hold.

Time management is not magic. Even with very careful management, it is clear from the president's diary that each day in the White House was brimful. And yet, he managed to be in bed by 11:00.

LESSON 153
MAKE HISTORY

"Men make history. History does not make the man."

—Quoted in Margaret Truman, *Harry S. Truman*

What distinguishes a leader from the led? Most of us are content—or resigned—to be either the victims or the beneficiaries of circumstance. In contrast, a leader understands that circumstance is the product of human action and is determined therefore to take a hand in creating that product. Truman, an avid student of biography and history, understood that by entering politics, he was getting into history—or, more accurately, into the history-making business. For him, this was as true when he was a Missouri county judge (the equivalent of a county commissioner) as it was when he became leader of the free world. Therein lies the significance for us of his observation that men make history, not history the man. For "history" is not just the history of the world or the history of the nation. It is also *local* history: the history of the county, the town, the neighborhood, the block, the enterprise, the company, the department, the family. In any of these realms we may choose to become a leader by accepting the truth of Truman's observation and resolving to take a hand in creating history, the circumstances in which we live and work.

The alternative is to accept whatever we find as we find it, to drift, as it were, with the prevailing current. When you embark on a new career or even just a new job in a new place, you have a choice. You may either work and act in ways that define who you are, or let others define you. In either case, you *will* be defined. If you affirmatively define yourself, you will claim at least that much of a leadership role and will begin to make at least that portion of the history that immediately surrounds you. If, instead, you abandon yourself to drift, a history out of your hands will indeed make you. Or, as the case may be, unmake you.

CHAPTER 12

RECKONING

LESSON 154
LOOK IN THE MIRROR

"In your column this morning, you speak of gross and costly blunders of the Truman Administration in foreign policy. Wish you would be specific and name them."

—Unsent letter to Arthur Krock, *New York Times* Washington correspondent, September 11, 1952

Harry Truman had a formidable reputation for speaking his mind, whether invited to do so or not. But even Truman sometimes held his tongue—or his pen. From time to time throughout his presidency, typically when something of the moment particularly bothered him, he wrote starkly candid letters and then decided not to send them. When *New York Times* Washington correspondent Arthur Krock mentioned in his column "gross and costly blunders of the Truman Administration in foreign policy," the president wrote a letter, which he then filed away. This unsent challenge to Krock is a rare glimpse of just how Truman evaluated himself. Unlike Krock, he was "specific," resorting to an enumeration of the facts:

Dear Arthur:

In your column this morning, you speak of gross and costly blunders of the Truman Administration in foreign policy. Wish you would be specific and name them.

Was the salvation of Greece and Turkey a blunder?

Was the Berlin Airlift a blunder? Was the economic recovery of free Europe with our assistance a blunder? Was the military rehabilitation and strengthening of the free world a blunder? Was the European Alliance (N.A.T.O.) a blunder? Was the rehabilitation of the Philippine Republic a blunder? Were the Japanese Treaty and the Pacific Agreements blunders?

Chiang Kai-shek's downfall was his own doing. His field Generals surrendered the equipment we gave him to the Commies and used his own arms and ammunition to overthrow him. Only an American Army of 2,000,000 men could have saved him and that would have been World War III.

Now where and what are the blunders?

Foreign policy has been costly. But World War III would be ten times as costly.

The appropriations for Greece and Turkey and the Marshall Plan and also for the Military Plan were voted by bipartisan majorities in Congress, which made them approved National Policies.

The Treaties were overwhelmingly approved.

I've always thought Arthur Krock to be intellectually honest. But when you contribute to the breakup of the foreign policy of the United States, you help bring on World War III. When you do it by misleading and untrue statements—well it is almost as bad for the country as McCarthyism.

You can disagree all you want on any subject, farm, labor, monetary, debt control or foreign policy and I won't care at all—if you tell the truth.

Evaluate performance, most of all your own, by the most objective measures you can find. An enumeration of achievements is a good start toward an honest evaluation.

LESSON 156
PITFALLS OF POWER

"There are three things that get a man."

—Letter to his cousin Ethel Noland, January 2, 1953

"Alexander the Great, Augustus Caesar, Jenghis Khan, Louis XIV, Napoleon nor any other of the great historical figures had the power or the world influence of the President of the U.S.A.," Truman remarked in a letter to his cousin Ethel Noland on January 2, 1953, little more than two weeks before the end of his presidency. "It bears down on a country boy. But I'm coming home Jan. 20th, 1953, and, I hope, pull a Cincinnatus, who was old G. Washington's ideal."

And Cincinnatus was clearly Truman's ideal as well: the leader who, his mission accomplished, quietly retired, seeking no further glory or power. Too many leaders, even the greatest, were dominated by fatal flaws. Truman continued:

> There are three things that get a man. No. 1 is Power—Alexander, Julius Caesar, Jenghis Khan, Tamerlane, Napoleon I. No. 2 is ambition for high social recognition. That is all tinsel and fake. No. 3 is appetite or inability to exercise physical restraint.
>
> Alexander—too much wine at the wrong time.
>
> Caesar—too much trust in ladies and what he thought were friends.

Napoleon—ideas of grandeur, his "star" and no control over his passions.

Nothing counted more on Truman's leadership scorecard than character.

Appendix

A TRUMAN TIMELINE

1884	8 May: Truman born, Lamar, Missouri
1885	Family moves to farm near Harrisonville, Missouri
1887	Family moves to farm near Grandview, Missouri
1890	Family moves to 619 Crysler Street, Independence, Missouri; Harry meets Bess Wallace at the Sunday school of the First Presbyterian Church
1900	Serves as a page at the Democratic National Convention, Kansas City
1901	Graduates from Independence High School
1902–1906	Works briefly in mail room of *Kansas City Star*, then as a timekeeper on a Santa Fe Railroad construction project, as a clerk for the National Bank of Commerce in Kansas City (to which he moved), and finally as a bookkeeper for Union National Bank
1905–1911	Served in Battery B, Missouri National Guard
1906	Moved to the Truman farm near Grandview, Missouri, to help operate it
1914	2 November: John Truman (father) dies; Harry Truman takes over farm; appointed road overseer in southern half of Washington Township
1915	Appointed postmaster of Grandview; loses money in a zinc-mining venture
1916	Is a founder of an oil-drilling company, which dissolves in 1919, having broken even
1917	June: Elected first lieutenant of Battery F, 2nd Missouri Artillery

	August: Sworn into regular army as member of 129th Field Artillery regiment
	September: Assigned to Camp Doniphan, Fort Sill, Oklahoma; with sergeant Eddie Jacobson, operates a post canteen
1918	13 April: Arrives in France
	May: Promoted to captain
	11 July: Assigned command, Battery D, 129th Field Artillery regiment, 35th Division
	6 September: First combat, in Vosges Mountains
	11 November: Armistice
1919	9 April: Departs Europe
	6 May: Discharged
	28 June: Marries Elizabeth (Bess) Wallace
	November: Opens haberdashery with Eddie Jacobson, 104 West 12th Street, Kansas City
1922	Haberdashery fails in a business recession; Truman refuses to file for bankruptcy, pledging to pay his debt dollar for dollar; endorsed by political boss T. J. Pendergast, elected eastern judge, Jackson County Court
1923–1925	Attends Kansas City School of Law
1924	Defeated for reelection as county judge; cofounds Community Savings and Loan Association, Independence, serving as general manager until 1932
1925–1926	Membership salesman, Kansas City Automobile Club
1926	Elected presiding judge (functions as county executive), Jackson County Court; serves two terms, to 1934
1928	Launches bond issue to build 224 miles of paved county highways and a county hospital
1931	Obtains new bond issues for more highways and other public buildings
1933	Appointed federal reemployment director for Missouri
1934	6 November: Elected to U.S. Senate

1937	Appointed vice-chairman, subcommittee of the Interstate Commerce Committee to investigate American railroad finances
1938	Helps draft Civil Aeronautics Act of 1938
1939	Cosponsors bill to place railroads under the Interstate Commerce Commission; as member of Military Subcommittee of the Appropriations Committee, tours key defense installations
1940	5 November: Reelected to Senate
1941	Successfully sponsors creation of Senate Special Committee to Investigate the National Defense Program ("Truman Committee"), which he chairs
1942	15 January: Truman Committee presents First Annual Report; instrumental in replacing Office of Production Management with a more powerful War Production Board
1943	8 February: Truman Committee responsible for saving about $11 billion
	8 March: Appears on cover of *Time* magazine
1944	7 November: Elected vice president
1945	29 January: Against political advice, attends funeral of the disgraced Thomas J. Pendergast
1945	12 April: Sworn in as 33rd U.S. president on the death of FDR
	25 April: Opens (via radio address) the United Nations Charter Conference
	May: Orders federal seizure of coal mines to prevent national strike
	8 May: War in Europe ends (V-E Day)
	17 July–2 August: Attends Potsdam Conference with Stalin and Churchill (succeeded by Clement Attlee) to lay out the postwar world
	6 August: Atomic bomb dropped on Hiroshima, Japan; another dropped on Nagasaki, 9 August

14 August: Japan surrenders (V-J Day), ending World War II

6 September: Presents legislative program to expand FDR's New Deal

1946   17 January: Resolves major nationwide steel strike

20 February: Employment Act of 1946 establishes Council of Economic Advisers

24 May: Proposes strong federal measures to end national strike of railroad trainmen and engineers; strike ends the next day

20 September: Replaces dissident Secretary of Commerce Henry A. Wallace with W. Averell Harriman

5 November: Midterm elections return Republican majorities to Congress

21 November–5 December: Showdown with United Mine Workers president John L. Lewis; miners return to work, 5 December

1947   7 January: James L. Byrnes resigns as secretary of state; replaced by George C. Marshall, 21 January

12 March: Requests major appropriation from Congress to "contain" spread of communism in Greece and Turkey, thereby inaugurating the Truman Doctrine

20 June: Veto of Taft-Hartley Bill as discriminatory against labor; Congress overrides veto, 23 June

26 July: Signs National Security Act of 1947, unifying the armed forces under what becomes the Department of Defense, creating an independent U.S. Air Force, and establishing the Central Intelligence Agency and the National Security Council

1948   31 January: Recognizes the new state of Israel

2 February: Asks Congress for legislation to secure the rights of minorities—first federal civil rights legislation since Reconstruction

3 April: Signs Foreign Assistance Act of 1948 to implement the Marshall Plan for postwar European recovery

25 June: Signs Displaced Persons Act to admit 205,000 European refugees to the United States

26 June: Orders Berlin Airlift

15 July: Nominated as Democratic presidential candidate; support of party's civil rights plank provokes walkout of Alabama and Mississippi delegates

15 July: Calls majority Republican Congress into special session on 26 July ("Turnip Day") to act on housing, civil rights, and price controls; Congress adjourns 7 August, having passed almost no legislation

6 September–30 October: Series of epic whistle-stop campaigns

2 November: Stuns pollsters by defeating Republican Thomas E. Dewey

1949   5 January: Proposes the "Fair Deal" economic policy

20 January: In inaugural address, proposes what becomes the Point Four Program to aid underdeveloped nations

20–21 January: Dean Acheson succeeds George Marshall as secretary of state

12 May: Soviet blockade of West Berlin ends

24 August: Proclaims North Atlantic Pact, which creates North Atlantic Treaty Organization (NATO)

1950   26 June: Orders U.S. air and naval forces to aid South Korea in resisting Communist North Korean invasion; use of ground forces follows, 30 June

25 August: Orders seizure of railroads to prevent crippling nationwide strike

12 September: Louis A. Johnson resigns as secretary of defense; replaced by George C. Marshall, 21 September

15 October: Meeting on Wake Island with General

Douglas MacArthur, supreme commander of United Nations forces in Korea

1 November: Attempted assassination by two Puerto Rican nationalists

16 December: Proclaims national emergency after China enters Korean War

1951   11 April: Relieves MacArthur for insubordination; MacArthur replaced by Lieutenant General Matthew B. Ridgway

15 June: Signs India Emergency Food Aid Act, lending nation $190 million

1952   2 January: Initiates sweeping reform of Bureau of Internal Revenue, which becomes Internal Revenue Service

8 April: Orders federal seizure of steel mills to avert a national strike; seizure declared unconstitutional, 2 June

1953   20 January: After attending inauguration of Dwight D. Eisenhower, returns to Independence, Missouri

1953–1955   Composes two volumes of memoirs, published in 1955 and 1956

1955   8 May: Breaks ground for privately financed Harry S. Truman Library; library completed in 1956

11 May–3 July: Triumphant tour of Europe

1959   27–29 April: Speaks and conducts seminar at Columbia University, New York

1960   Truman's *Mr. Citizen*, book about life after the White House, published

20 August: Announces support of John F. Kennedy candidacy; campaigns 8 October–4 November

1963   29 May: Statue in Athens, Greece, honors Truman as one of Greece's "greatest benefactors"

1964   First of 26 programs broadcast in the television series *Decision: The Conflicts of Harry S. Truman*

1972   26 December: Dies, at age 88, after a brief illness

1982   18 October: Bess Truman dies, at age 97

Recommended Reading

THE SOURCES OF
WHEN THE BUCK STOPS WITH YOU

The Truman years were among the most eventful and complex of the twentieth century. The following books served as the primary sources of the information and quotations in *When the Buck Stops with You* and are indispensable to anyone seriously interested in the life and career of Harry S. Truman or modern American history.

Acheson, Dean. *Present at the Creation: My Years in the State Department.* London: Hamish Hamilton, 1969.

Daniels, Jonathan. *The Man of Independence.* Philadelphia: Lippincott, 1950.

Donovan, Robert J., ed. *The Words of Harry Truman.* New York: Newmarket, 1984.

Ferrell, Robert H., ed. *The Autobiography of Harry S. Truman.* Boulder: Colorado Associated University Press, 1980.

———. *Dear Bess: The Letters from Harry to Bess Truman, 1910–1959.* New York: Norton, 1983.

———. *Harry S. Truman: A Life.* Columbia: University of Missouri Press, 1994.

———. *Off the Record: The Private Papers of Harry S. Truman.* Pub. 1980. Reprint. Columbia: University of Missouri Press, 1997.

Frost, Elizabeth. *The Bully Pulpit: Quotations from American Presidents.* New York: Facts on File, 1988.

Gallen, David, ed. *The Quotable Truman.* New York: Carroll and Graf, 1994.

Hechler, Ken. *Working with Truman: A Personal Memoir of the White House Years.* New York: Putnam, 1982.

Henning, Chuck, ed. *The Wit and Wisdom of Politics.* Golden, Colo.: Fulcrum, 1992.

Hersey, John. *Aspects of the Presidency.* New Haven and New York: Ticknor and Fields, 1980.

Hillman, William. *Mr. President.* New York: Farrar, Straus and Young, 1952.

Keyes, Ralph. *The Wit and Wisdom of Harry Truman: A Treasury of Quotations, Anecdotes, and Observations.* New York: Gramercy Press, 1995.

Kirkendall, Richard S., ed. *The Harry S. Truman Encyclopedia.* Boston: G. K. Hall, 1989.

McCullough, David. *Truman.* New York: Simon and Schuster, 1992.

Miller, Merle, ed. *Plain Speaking: An Oral Biography of Harry S. Truman.* London: Gollancz, 1974.

Poen, Monte M., ed. *Strictly Personal and Confidential: The Letters Harry Truman Never Mailed.* Boston: Little, Brown, 1984.

Robbins, Charles. *Last of His Kind: An Informal Portrait of Harry S. Truman.* New York: Morrow, 1979.

Rossiter, Clinton. *The American Presidency.* New York: Harcourt, Brace and World, 1960.

Sertel, T. S., ed. *The Quotable Harry S. Truman.* New York: Berkeley, 1975.

Smith, Timothy, ed. *Merriman Smith's Book of Presidents: A White House Memoir.* New York: Norton, 1972.

Steinberg, Alfred. *The Man from Missouri: The Life and Times of Harry S. Truman.* New York: Putnam, 1962.

Thompson, Kenneth W., ed. *Portraits of American Presidents: The Truman Presidency.* Lanham, Md.: University Press of America, 1984.

Thomson, David S. *HST: A Pictorial Biography.* New York: Grossett & Dunlap, 1973.

Truman, Harry S. *Memoirs, Volume One: Year of Decisions.* Garden City, N.Y.: Doubleday, 1955.

———. *Memoirs, Volume Two: Years of Trial and Hope.* Garden City, N.Y.: Doubleday, 1956.

———. *Mr. Citizen.* New York: Bernard Geis, 1960.

———. *Truman Speaks.* New York: Columbia University Press, 1960.

———. *Public Papers of the Presidents of the United States. Harry S. Truman. Containing the Public Messages, Speeches and Statements of the President.* Washington, D.C.: Government Printing Office, 1945–1953.

Truman, Margaret. *Harry S. Truman.* New York: Morrow, 1973.

———, ed. *Letters from Father: The Truman Family's Personal Correspondence.* New York: Arbor House, 1981.

———, ed. *Where the Buck Stops: The Personal and Private Writings of Harry S. Truman.* New York: Warner, 1989.

United States Congress. *Memorial Services in the Congress of the United States and Tributes in Eulogy of Harry S. Truman, Late a President of the United States.* Washington, D.C.: Government Printing Office, 1973.

Index